BECOME AN AGILE PROJECT MANAGER

Beginner's Guide to Mastering Agile Project Management with Scrum, Kanban, Scrumban, Lean, Six Sigma, and Extreme Programming

© Copyright Ready Set Agile! 2020 – All rights reserved.

The content contained within this book may not be reproduced, duplicated, or transmitted without direct written permission from the author or the publisher except for the use of brief quotations in a book review. Under no circumstances will any blame or legal responsibility be held against the publisher, or author, for any damages, reparation, or monetary loss due to the information contained within this book. Either directly or indirectly. You are responsible for your own choices, actions, and results.

Legal Notice:
This book is copyright protected. This book is only for personal use. You cannot amend, distribute, sell, use, quote or paraphrase any part, or the content within this book, without the consent of the author or publisher except for the use of brief quotations in a book review.

Disclaimer notice:
Please note the information contained within this book is for educational and entertainment purposes only. All effort has been executed to present accurate, up to date, and reliable, complete information. No warranties of any kind are declared or implied. Readers acknowledge that the author is not engaging in the rendering of legal, financial, medical, or professional advice. The content within this book has been derived from various sources. Please consult a licensed professional before attempting any techniques outlined in this book.
By reading this book, the reader agrees that under no circumstances is the author responsible for any losses, direct or indirect, which are incurred as a result of the use of the information contained within this book, including, but not limited to,–errors, omissions, or inaccuracies.

BECOME AN AGILE PROJECT MANAGER

Beginner's Guide to Mastering Agile Project Management with Scrum, Kanban, Scrumban, Lean, Six Sigma, and Extreme Programming

2020

TABLE OF CONTENTS

7 BEST PRACTICES of the Agile Project Manager

Each practice includes:

- 2 to 4 critical actions
- Easy but powerful steps
- Activities that will make you a pro PM

To download your checklist, click and visit the link:

rsagile.activehosted.com/f/13

READY
SET
AGILE!

INTRODUCTION

ARE you dreaming about a better career? You know you've got leadership skills, and you're ready to put them to work. You may be on a project management team right now. Are you frustrated with the work you're doing, or disappointed in your project manager's lack of success? Do you feel like you're not able to change the environment as planned?

Many people hold back from applying for a project manager position because they're not sure if they have the technical skills required, or not sure they have the background to become a project manager. However, being on a project often makes it easier to figure out what's going wrong or why the project isn't as successful as it could be.

Have you ever noticed that you can see what needs to be improved on the project management (PM) team? Good news! You now have the great opportunity to become an excellent agile project manager. Why? Because you have what most project managers lack—a proper understanding of the work.

Leading a project is an excellent way to effect change, make products and processes better, and work more closely with other people. It also helps people exercise their leadership skills. This book is all about leading projects, and not just ordinary projects—the most successful projects, from small start-ups to the largest corporations in the world.

Your background may not be in leadership or project management. You might be an IT developer, designer, accountant, product developer, admin, sales representative, human resources specialist, or even just fresh out of school. It doesn't matter. You can start from wherever you are and use this book to build up your project management skills and techniques.

Better yet, you don't have to spend years of your life studying project management to be a good project manager. You'll need to understand the basic techniques, which is what I will be discussing in this book. More importantly, you'll learn about the different roles available in agile project management and gain a mastery that you can then bring toward becoming a project manager.

Some people ask me if it's OK to start as a project manager without any prior experience on projects. The answer's yes, for two reasons. One is that you've already participated in projects in your studies and personal life. It might have been studying for your final exam, moving to another town, constructing something from Lego pieces, or building a sports team with your friends.

The second reason is that the crucial piece of being a project manager is leadership ability. Yes, you need a solid knowledge of the different roles of the team and how to work together. However, you don't necessarily have to be an expert in any of them. What you need is the capacity for leading the team and developing the buy-in from all the stakeholders. It doesn't matter what industry or position you're currently in, as long as you want to lead a team. It can happen much faster than waiting years until you become a team leader in your department.

I'll discuss being an effective project manager in my next book. For the moment, the focus is on developing the confidence to step into that project manager role. This book will provide you with the fundamentals so that you'll have the knowledge to be an agile project manager. The world loves a team leader, so your aptitude for this can take you far.

At this point, you might be wondering why I'm so convinced that being an agile project manager is a career worth pursuing. Projects are the primary way that companies create new things and improve existing ones. Here, I reveal to you the first secret: project manage-

ment is the most important tool that companies use to achieve their strategic goals. Effective project management practices are present in all successful companies, regardless of size and industry.

Over the years, experts have developed several project management methodologies as they searched for better ways to bring new products to life. So far, the most successful method is known as agile project management (APM). It's a system that responds to changes and adapts quickly, and it is applied in all industries and to all project sizes. Collaborations with clients occur faster and at a deeper level.

Organizations and individuals already use APM methodologies such as Scrum, Kanban, and Six Sigma. I'll discuss these frameworks later in the book, so you will also have familiarity with them. You'll discover the most common PM software tools that are used today and learn the advantages and disadvantages of each. These tools will help simplify your transition and provide easier growth in your new field. As a bonus, you will receive a selection of most popular PM tools that you can use for free for your personal projects.

In this book, I will be providing you with an in-depth discussion of all the principles involved in APM practice. I'll unlock the hidden secrets as to why certain models are better than others, and why one size does not fit all. I will also show you how you can blend them to find a model that works well with each situation. Since we learn best with examples, I will provide real-life examples as well.

I've seen employees working on projects who look at the inefficiencies of their project managers/Scrum masters and believe they could do better. However, they rarely take the chance to level up. It's unfortunate because being a project manager is lucrative today and can lead to an exciting career with lots of different projects and teams to work with in the future.

Leading a project indeed requires technical, leadership, and communication skills. If done incorrectly, it might lead to the project's failure. This reason could have likely been why you have been avoiding trying project management, even when you would have done a great job.

Don't worry about the past. I will show you APM methods, approaches, and roles. You might not think you're ready right now to make the leap, but people without any previous experience or education in PM methods do very well in the profession just by following some simple steps that you'll find in this book. Learning more about project management, especially APM, you'll develop the confidence you need to make that switch.

You might be wondering how I can be so sure that someone with little experience can step into this type of leadership role. I've been in project management for years in several different positions and teams. As a project manager, I've had the opportunity to manage several projects, ranging from small start-up projects to large, cross-divisional ones that lasted several years. I've seen projects succeed, and I've also seen them fail. I want to help new project managers learn what I've learned, without having to go through everything I did to acquire that knowledge. Throughout my years in the industry, I have picked up vital lessons, and I can't wait to share them with you.

By using my experience to guide you, you'll have the basics that you need to understand the various methodologies and when to use them. You'll find which ones work best for you. More importantly, by acquiring this background, you'll be confident in your newfound ability to lead teams.

Many people have used the lessons that I'm providing to make better lives for themselves. My readers have gone from IT support to effecting change and delivering results as project managers. Some of them started in administrative roles in the company and went on to successfully lead their teams. They were able to achieve this feat from the simple steps and approaches discussed in this book. When

they first came to my teachings, many of them weren't sure they had "the right stuff" to be project managers. However, they learned and grew into their new roles. For me, it was like seeing a miracle. People without self-confidence became leaders and helped not only themselves but their entire team.

Why would you stay in a job that doesn't satisfy you? That won't give you the opportunity to develop your leadership and communication capabilities? That doesn't pay you enough for your work? If you want to launch yourself into this new and exciting career, the time to act is now. Read this book to the very end, and you will see yourself becoming the project manager you have always dreamed of being.

In addition, you can use APM principles in everyday life to manage your work. Have you ever had a goal, planned for it, used feedback to improve your chances, and eventually achieved it? You've practiced project management already! Whether it's planning a vacation, building a house, or even developing a healthy and fit body. Putting APM to work will be a life-changer for your career and personal life. Why wait? Start reading now! I've created the Ready, Set, Agile! methodology, which you can easily remember and apply everywhere. You'll have the agile methodology right where you need it.

Are you **Ready** and **Set** to become the **Agile** project manager? Then read on as we start the journey together!

CHAPTER 1

WHAT IS PROJECT MANAGEMENT?

TO begin, you will need a clear understanding of what project management actually is. Fundamentally, it's about achieving the goal of a specific project. There are finite timelines and budgets for the specified deliverables. The application of methodology, skills, experience, and knowledge will accomplish the required objectives for the project, as mapped out by the team responsible for the results. You can distinguish project management from "regular" management by the measurable goals and a definite end date.

What is a Project?

In brief, it's an effort to create something new or modify what is already in existence. Whether it's software, cars, or packaging materials, a project can also be a service. In safety consulting, a project might be to reduce the number of workplace safety incidents at a specific location by 25% or reduce the costs of a worker's compensation claims by 50%. By contrast, a process occurs repetitively.

A project may be described in terms of outcomes or benefits, and it's usually bound within a certain timeframe and budget. It's successful if it meets the criteria determined at the outset of the process.

A project is always unique. For example, designing a new type of engine for an electric car can be defined as a project. Once the project is completed successfully, the engine maker would produce the engines in a factory according to the process that was designed in the project. Making the engine is a *process* because it's a repetitive task, but developing the design itself is a *project*.

Projects differ in complexity. One might be simple and require few tasks with just one person. Others are genuinely complex and may require collaboration from a large team. Take a look around you—the cell phone on your desk started as a project as well as your TV. The roads on which we drive all started as projects.

Even if you've never led a project in the office, you've probably managed a project before. You've redecorated your room, changed an old procedure to make it more efficient, or found the best way to take notes during an important call. Managing projects is not only for those who've acquired the title of "project manager." In the beginning, you have a goal. For that goal, you decide what needs to be done to bring about the results you want, and then you would execute the plan. In the end, you have your result.

It doesn't matter who you are or what you do. If you have a goal and plan to see it through, you need to know how to manage it. Whether you're an IT professional, engineer, creative designer, or director, project management is critical for achieving your planned objectives.

Stakeholders

Every project has stakeholders with some kind of "stake" in the outcome of the project. They may either be internal to the company or external. Typically, the different stakeholders of a project would also have different objectives.

- **Sponsor**

  Sponsors often have the most significant influence on a project's success or failure. They're typically a higher-level manager or director and have the highest interest in the project's outcome. This person is behind allocating the budget for the project and smooths the way for affected departments and managers to accept the changes that come along with the project.

- **Project Manager**

  This person leads the project team. Their responsibilities vary according to what type of PM is in use. In general, they're the ones who must deliver the results on time and budget. They develop a plan for the project in conjunction with stakeholders and the team. They're also the ones who manage the individual team members.

- **Team Members**

  The project team also consists of these individuals. Some work on the whole project, whereas others join only certain phases and tasks as specialists. They perform the project tasks and (if using the appropriate framework) make decisions and adjustments on the fly. Everyone on the project management team wants the project to be successful; thus, it's not just good for the company, but also the member's career.

The members should collaborate successfully and master their own project tasks.

- **Management**

  Managers have their goals and key performance indicators (KPIs) that must be met, and they also need to adhere to budgets. They must allocate resources efficiently to complete a project on time to ensure that their other priorities are also accounted for.

- **Company Shareholders**

  They're not typically as involved in the details of the project. A successful project for them is one that makes the company more profitable and helps achieve strategic goals.

- **Affected Departments**

  The new project may make another department's work more efficient or allow them to be more productive. However, if the members of the department need to make changes to accommodate the new project, they may not welcome it. In this case, the department must cooperate, despite seeing no benefits from the project. Therefore, management and others must continue to lay the groundwork for acceptance and buy-in during the process.

- **Customer**

  Customers may be internal, external, or both. Internal customers include other departments—which may be marketing, sales, or finance—who will use new software or benefit from process improvement.

External customers are outside the organization. For example, a hotel company may request a team to develop a new online reservation system for them. The customers in the hotel organization may range from senior executives to the junior staff who would use the software.

- **Users**

  These stakeholders will use the product or service being developed by the project team. Their specific requirements must be addressed by the project for it to be successful. Users will want their needs met for a reasonable price.

- **Subcontractors**

  The company may hire outside contractors to develop a portion of the project. They may have in-depth product knowledge or experience in the industry or be experts on a specific item of project management. They have to deliver their part of the job at the agreed quality and time.

- **Public**

  Members of the community and relatives and friends of the customers may also be stakeholders in a project. The company's products must have a good reputation.

- **Regulatory (or other) Authorities**

  These stakeholders might be customers, outside users, or even outside authorities whose approval may be required. They will want the project to conform to their guidelines.

Sometimes, stakeholders overlap. A user of the software is often also the customer. The manager may also be a sponsor. In smaller companies, one person would perform several roles. In private life, this is pretty common! For example, when you want to remodel your house, you would be the owner, project manager, customer, user, and sponsor. You hire a contractor to do the work, who usually hires subcontractors of their own.

Clearly defining the stakeholders in a given project helps define and structure the parameters of the project, along with what the deliverables need to be because each stakeholder has an interest in its success.

Nine Management Areas

To understand the function of a project manager, you'll need to know about the following nine key areas. Bear in mind that you don't have to be an expert in all of these–that's what your team is for! However, you do need to have a general knowledge of each, so you can know if one key area isn't being attended to properly.

1. Integration Management

There are normally many tasks going on at the same time. As a project manager, you'll need to manage all these and understand how they work together. The leader of one task may not understand how their task fits in with their colleague's, but you will need to know how all the pieces of the puzzle fit together.

It's similar to being the head coach of a football team. You would need to coordinate the defensive team, offensive team, along with special teams. Each of these has their own coach and their own ways of practicing, and you would be responsible for putting it all on the field and making sure all the parts work together.

2. Scope Management

At the outset, you would define the scope of the project. You and the team would outline the work and document the plan. Identify the deliverables, what problem(s) the team will solve, and the expected timeline.

What often happens, if no one is paying attention to the scope, is that the project starts to become bigger and bigger. This is known as "scope creep." Suddenly, there's another deliverable or problem. Team members are diverted to these other issues outside the original scope, and the project isn't delivered on time. In the worst-case scenario, the original problems don't even get solved because the team is trying to solve the new ones that have arisen!

Suppose your project is to reduce worker's compensation claims at the main factory by 25%. Once the work is started, you discover there's another warehouse where workers are being injured. If you start work at the warehouse, now the work at the original factory is no longer being completed, and the worker's comp claims there either stay the same or get worse. Now the client's unhappy, and you can't deliver on time or budget.

3. Time Management

Have you ever remodeled your home? Did the project happen on time and budget? Probably not! Building contractors are notorious for this. How annoyed were you that you couldn't use your home for months because the work didn't get done on time? How angry did you get when you had to keep forking over money due to cost overruns? Would you ever use that contractor again?

Of course not. If you want to keep the client happy, you will need to deliver the specified product at the agreed time! It's usually up to the project manager to keep an eye on the overall timeline. Is the team hitting the milestones? If not, why? Time management is key to developing a schedule and measuring whether tasks are completed on time.

4. Cost Management

Similarly, no one likes it when you keep coming back to them while presenting your hand out for more money. Team members may not have a good sense of the budget and be inclined to spend a lot of money, especially if it belongs to someone else!

The process is broken down into particular activities. With the team's input, the project manager estimates the timeline and how much it will cost. From there, they would develop a budget with a specific amount of work for each team. The project manager would monitor the project along the way to ensure the budget is being followed.

There are two types of costs: external costs represent fees for using contractors, purchasing material, IT and other equipment, specialized software, team building activities, external testing of marketing and product features, and regulatory fees. Internal costs are mainly salaries and usage of other company resources, equipment, and materials. The controlling department usually calculates the average hourly salary for your project.

5. Procurement

To complete the project, you'll probably need to purchase materials or services from third party suppliers. You would have estimated the cost earlier, but you will also need a plan for procuring these items.

There may be rules in your company about the process of ordering the supplies you need. The procurement department often buys in bulk, so they can provide these supplies at a much lower cost than if you ordered just for your team. You'll probably need to have your list ready in advance so that the department can buy everything most cost-effectively.

6. Quality Assurance (QA)

A high-quality product meets the user's needs with few to no defects or deficiencies. Monitoring the product along the way for quality will help deliver a reliable product. In software, many teams have associates assigned to test the product, along with ensuring all bugs are correctly resolved. Likewise, the Quality Assurance (QA) team may review the list of customer requirements to ensure that the product meets the minimum baselines. They may also test to ensure it meets ISO or other standards of the industry.

7. Risk Management

We all know that certain incidents may occur, as the future is filled with unknowns. However, most of the time, there are known risks that can be mitigated or eliminated. Having a plan to deal with different risks as they come up can help prevent the project management team from falling apart when something happens.

The concept is straightforward—develop a list of the risks that could foreseeably occur, then design steps that will eliminate or mitigate them. When something does happen, then you would execute your plans.

What's on the other side of the coin from risk? Opportunity. You will want to create a plan to take advantage of opportunities as they arise. The plan is the same as with risk management: identify potential opportunities that may arise and devise strategies that will allow you to take advantage of them. When they occur, execute the plan.

8. Human Resources (HR)

Hiring the right people for the team is crucial to success. The project manager will ideally be able to find the perfect people who can suit the roles best. This task may sometimes be a challenge because managers don't like to lose their best players to another "team," even when that team is making improvements. However, a project manager will have the opportunity to create their dream team at the start of each new project.

The project manager would also need to provide encouragement to the team and help them find effective ways to collaborate.

An integral part of managing people is handling conflict. When resolved healthily, conflict can be great for the team, as it ensures everyone's voice is heard. Otherwise, the team may fall victim to "groupthink," in which no dissent is tolerated; thus, new and useful ideas never come to light.

A good team challenges each other to be their best, and the project manager would help facilitate this.

9. Communication

Communication is also essential when working with a group of people. In addition to using software tools so all parts of the project are transparent to everyone involved, project managers need to be able to communicate with their team and facilitate strong connections between team members.

Once again, imagine a football team on the field. When all the players know the play and the quarterback has communicated it, each player would know where they should be on the field and what their environment would probably look like. They will be better equipped to spot opportunities because they know where their teammates are and what the goal of the play is.

In a new scenario, imagine that no one knows the play. The quarterback has an idea in their head of what they want to do, but they don't communicate it to anyone else. Their receivers have no idea where to go, and the defensive line doesn't know who they should be protecting. Is it a running play? A passing play? No one knows. As you can probably picture, there would be chaos on the field.

And it's the same on a project team when not everyone is on the same page, or if communication with other stakeholders is weak. For example, the sponsor must be informed on progress and status every week to make the right and timely decisions.

Tools of Project Management

Project management uses many easy-to-learn but powerful tools in its execution. These tools are an integral part of project management software, which I will present in chapter four.

Remember that the tools are just that–tools. They're not the goal in and of themselves, and PM isn't about the tools either.

"At its most fundamental, project management is about people getting things done." –Dr. Martin Barnes, APM President 2003-2012

- **Mind Map**

  These are helpful, especially at the beginning of a task when the team is throwing out ideas. Each idea can then be linked where appropriate. It's a less formal structure than trees or charts, so it may spur some additional creativity that you may not otherwise see.

- **Work Breakdown Structure (WBS) Chart**

  The Work Breakdown Structure (WBS) is a way to picture the scope of the project. It's based on a tree structure, with the overall goal at the top broken down into smaller tasks and projects below it. It's similar to a flowchart.

- **Gantt Chart**

  Henry Gantt is regarded as one of the forefathers of project management. His most notable contribution to the field is his introduction of the visual scheduling diagram known as the "Gantt" or "waterfall" charts. Introduced in the 1920s, it was a radical innovation in the field. Gantt proposed that, if visual timelines were used to plot tasks as lines with their durations, every party to the project would see the schedule more clearly.

  People understand graphical information very quickly. With this type of chart, it's easy to see how one activity would flow down to the next like a waterfall. It's simple yet powerful, and even after a century is still very popular.

- **Project Evaluation and Review Technique (PERT) Chart**

  Similar to a Gantt chart, the Project Evaluation and Review Technique (PERT) provides a visual picture of where the project stands for any number of tasks and milestones. It shows the relationship between activities too, which the Gantt chart does not.

- **Workflow Management**

  You'll need to be able to track the tasks and sub-projects as you go. With today's complex teams and variables, software is the easiest and best way to do this.

- **Calendar/Timeline**

  Everyone needs to know when their tasks are due. You can use digital or paper calendars, or you can create an in-depth timeline that shows all the important dates together.

- **To-Do Tracking**

  To-do lists are some of the most straightforward strategies people use to prioritize their workloads. Knowing what needs t o be done each day can help keep each member of the team focused, especially since project management has a deadline. Thus, each team member understands what must be done by the end of the day to stay on schedule.

- **Checklists**

  Having automated checklists ensure that tasks don't get dropped or anything important is omitted. Once the appropriate person completes a step, then the task would move to the next designated member.

- **Time Tracking**

  To be paid, your client or manager may require you to track the hours that your team works. Each team member must document their hours, which should then be compared to the budget. As you might imagine, software/automation helps significantly with this task! Once you've determined whether a team member is over or under budget, you can make a plan of action to bring everyone back on schedule.

- **Collaboration**

  Your team may not all be in one place, so you'll need web conferences to stay in touch. Email isn't always the best way to communicate, and being able to instant message other team members or ask questions on a forum will help smooth out the path. Modern collaboration software will contain many of the above tools in one place.

Key Takeaways

Project management isn't just a skill for business–it's something that everyone can use in their daily lives. When considering corporate projects, many different stakeholders will need to be considered to deliver a successful project.

- We learned what a project is.
- Everybody has managed a project, whether they realize it or not.
- Stakeholders, both external and internal, have interests in a project, and identifying them will help project managers define their deliverables.
- There are nine management areas that a project manager must use for a successful project.
- There are great tools–many of which are automated or digital–that a project manager can use to keep track of the project while facilitating communication.

In the next chapter, you will learn about the standard project management methodology, known as waterfall project management.

READY
SET
AGILE!

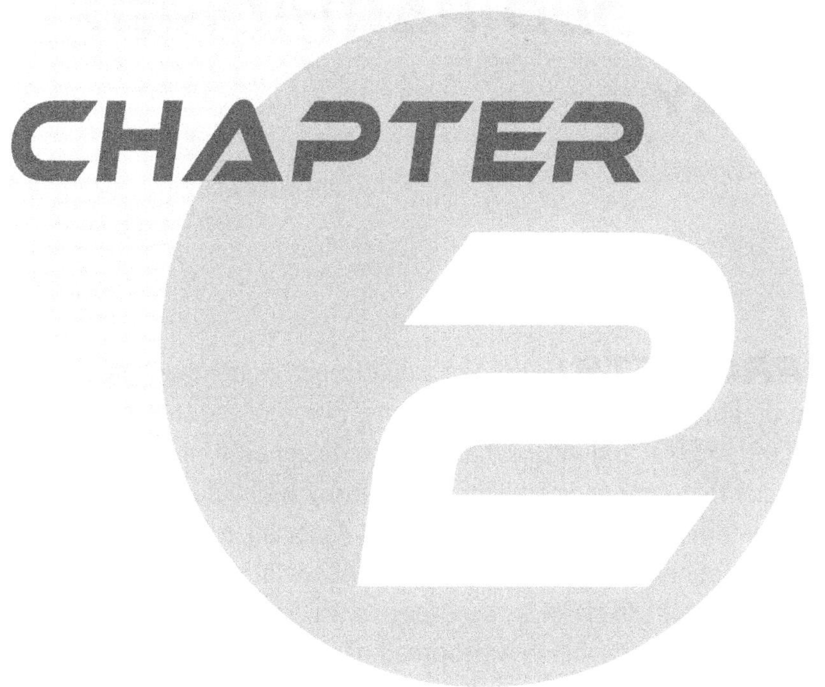
CHAPTER
2

WATERFALL: PROJECT MANAGEMENT THE OLD-FASHIONED WAY

PROJECTS have been around much longer than the official project management profession has. Some of the tools, such as Gantt, PERT, and WBS charts, were designed to make projects easier to handle and distill their complexity, well before 1965 when the International Project Management Association was established (International Project Management Association [IPMA], n.d.).[1] The original style of PM is now known as waterfall or traditional project management. It's still in widespread use today because there now exist many projects that are well suited to this methodology.

Waterfall PM and How it Works

In this methodology, tasks and duties are specified completely in the planning stage, then spill down chronologically (thus, "waterfall"). Since it was the first method used, it's also known as traditional PM.

Phases of the project occur in chronological order. The second task can only start after the first task is completed, and so on. The plan for the entire project is decided upfront. It's typical in construction and manufacturing because these types of projects don't require many iterations or repeated steps, and the goal can be defined precisely in the beginning. Software developers use it less because the nature of software often requires changes and further specifications in the project as it goes along the timeline.

In the waterfall, the planning upfront is key to the success of the project. Because there is no iteration, it has to work right out of the gate. This requires extensive documentation and organization. It's highly structured since each stage must be completed before going on to the next.

Six Phases of Waterfall PM

As waterfall PM is a structured process, it would follow these six phases fairly closely. Some sources add in a conception or charter phase at the beginning to show seven elements. The conception stage may include a project charter, so all stakeholders are aligned on the purpose of the project. The charter includes the project scope, timeframe, budget, key stakeholders, and deliverables.

Waterfall projects tend to adhere to these stages in this specific order.

1. Requirements

What does the client need? The focus for a waterfall project is what will be delivered to the client in step five.

What does the team need to provide in the deliverable? What knowledge, services, and materials will they need?

When does the client need to have the product in their possession? Are there any constraints under which they're operating that will affect the team's performance, or that the team needs to take into account?

2. Design (Plan)

Given the requirements, now the team must plan how they will achieve the goal. They need to consider how the budget will be allocated among the different project stages, as well as the timeline.

The plan must account for every aspect of the deliverable because it's difficult to make changes along the way. Any change must be evaluated and approved. The entire plan has to be mapped out at this stage, including the timing of the start and end of each activity, staff allocation, and budget. The plan is, therefore, the roadmap, which is set in stone.

3. Implementation

Here's where the roadmap is painstakingly carried out. Once one stage is finished, the next may begin. The team is expected to adhere to the budget and timeline provided in the design stage. Whatever the deliverable is, it must be completed during this wave.

4. Testing/QA

Now that the deliverable is complete, it needs to be tested and run through quality assurance to ensure that it is up to the client's expectation level. Up until now, there has been no testing, so this would be the first chance to make sure it works. Whatever that means for the particular project.

5. Delivery

This one is pretty self-explanatory. Hopefully, the end product passed its QA tests and can be delivered to the client.

6. Maintenance

At this point, the team would rely on the customers to let them know if any real-world problems have occurred, so they can go back and fix it.

Project Team Members

Due to the highly structured nature of this type of project management, teams can be very large, with each team member having a discrete role to play.

The project manager is the leader, similar to a coach in terms of a football team. They communicate with stakeholders and, in some cases, with clients. They are also usually tasked with creating buy-in and facilitating communication with the team. Project managers help keep their players motivated and focused on the goal. They monitor the progress of the project, ensuring that the team stays on schedule and budget. They manage the reports and documentation (though they may not be writing the documents themselves.)

On a large team, in addition to the project manager, there may also be team leaders. They lead a sub-team within the broader project team as a whole. Instead of acting like the boss, this person would be more of a team facilitator. They model appropriate problem-solving behavior, help team members initiate action, listen to each member, coach them, and do some of the work themselves. Being in the field themselves is vital for maintaining team unity. They maneuver through political waters to get the job done.

Other team members typically have specific technical skills in areas like software development, market research, or finance. They also need to have problem-solving skills and be able to communicate with others. If there are politics involved, they'll escalate to the team leader or project manager as appropriate.

Software project teams also have developers responsible for writing the code in the implementation phase, and testers who run the QA in that stage. The business analyst writes the business strategies for the project and is on the team.

Outside the team, a project sponsor can be very helpful. They get buy-in at the highest levels of the organization and smooth over organizational obstacles. While this role isn't required or even always available, it can have a huge influence on whether a project succeeds.

Advantages of Waterfall

When you have a project that requires a relatively rigid structure, a lot of organization, and predictability, the waterfall method works very well. It's a suitable method when you know the scope, budget, and requirements, and especially when you've done similar projects and have a solid grasp on how long you need and how much it will cost. A low-risk project, such as a clone of something that already exists, is well-suited to this methodology. Also, if you have a hardship date, you might want to use waterfall. It is helpful when the requirements are unlikely to change during the course of the project.

However, it does not work well when you don't know what the final result will be exactly (which is common in software), or you need to run multiple tests or prototypes. If the industry standards change rapidly, or you know the end result depends on user feedback, you will need a more flexible methodology.

Software normally requires constant testing and the incorporation of user feedback, so it's better suited to agile or another, more iterative type of PM. On the other hand, someone who's building a bridge will need to get the project done right the first time, and waterfall would be great for that.

- **Prioritization**

  The critical path is identified with all the dependent tasks flowing into one another. It is clear which step to take next, and important tasks are highlighted.

- **Documentation**

  Planning ahead requires extensive documentation right from the beginning. This makes the process repeatable and clear to all team members.

- **Knowledge capture**

  As a result of all the required documentation, knowledge doesn't walk out the door along with a team member or after the project. Future teams working on similar problems can use the lessons learned of those who have gone before.

- **Clarity and predictability**

  The wave-by-wave process makes it easy for stakeholders without much technical skill to understand what's going on. Clients who are focused on the bottom line can see where the process is at any given time without much coaching from the team.

- **Ease of time management**

  Every team member knows what their deadlines are with waterfall PM. Every stage and each task is clearly defined. Each member can also work on more than one project at a time because they know when they will be required for each task.

- **Minimal client input (after planning)**

  Once the planning is complete, there will be no need for additional input beyond update meetings and the like. The entire project timeline is known from the start, and the client will understand what is happening when. There is no need to provide input after the whole framework is completed and ready to go.

- **Progress tracking**

  With defined stages, it is simple even for non-technical people to understand where the project is at any given time, and where it was supposed to be at that time. Gantt charts shine here because their color-coding makes it clear whether the task is on schedule or not.

- **Design quality**

  Knowing that there is no iteration, the team should understand that the entire project must be designed thoroughly before the first stage can begin work. Because the entire project is dependent on the original plan, it has to be of top quality right from the start.

Disadvantages of Waterfall

- **No room for error**

  Because everything is designed and estimated upfront, if something goes wrong, the entire project may be unable to complete, or the team will have to go back to the planning stage and start over completely. Needless to say, most clients will not be thrilled with the extra time and money such errors can cause!

- **QA comes too late**

  The quality assurance usually doesn't happen until the end of the project, when it's tested. If the testing fails, the team may need to go back to square one or scrap it altogether.

- **Lots of bugs in software development**

  Bugs follow from being unable to test during the process. At the end, when time is short and the team is scrambling to stay on schedule, the testing is often rushed as well. Therefore, bugs will not get caught in time.

- **Schedule failure**

  Once one stage fails to be completed on time, the entire rest of the project will be at risk for not coming in on schedule. Most projects don't have much time built in to catch up when one stage runs late.

- **Requirement failure**

  Clients, in many cases, don't know what they need exactly, though they often have a good sense of what they don't need. The clients could also want to solve their problem, but leave the solution to the supplier. In a rigid waterfall structure, the client is often surprised by the final product they received, or the team realizes they need the plan to be overhauled, the latter suggesting another massive infusion of time and money.

- **Change in priorities**

  As the coronavirus has shown us, circumstances and technologies change rapidly, even in a matter of weeks or months. In situations like these, clients and management are often forced

to change their strategies, leaving the project headed in the wrong direction.

- **Unexpected problems**

  There's no slack in either the budget or the timeline if something completely unforeseen occurs, which could delay the project or cause a budget overrun.

Waterfall Success Rate

Of course, all projects have varying degrees of complexity and different factors that contribute to their success or failure. A successful project is one that meets the original requirements in terms of scope, cost, and schedule. In the software industry, waterfall projects are successful 49% of the time. Their biggest flaw is that they tend to overrun on schedule. Other project management styles, such as agile, fare better: 2/3 agile projects overall succeed (Ambler, 2014).[2]

When the overall IT industry is considered, the statistics are more startling. Agile projects succeed 42% of the time, and waterfall only 26%. Interestingly, size does matter when it comes to project success! Large projects are more likely to fail than smaller ones. The agile methodology makes a big difference in the success rates of large and medium projects, far outpacing waterfall. Over time, fortunately, the success rate of all projects has improved (Mersino, 2019).[3]

Key Takeaways

Traditional project management is still necessary for some projects with a fixed scope and requirements that are unlikely to change over time. It's a hierarchical system that is well-suited to bureaucratic organizations that depend on command-and-control structures.

- Waterfall project management is the original PM process, which is still the right choice for many projects today.
- This methodology relies on completing one stage at a time in a linear fashion, without iterations or user feedback.
- Waterfall has six phases: requirements, design, implementation, testing, delivery, and maintenance.
- The project team consists of a project manager, team leader, and team members.
- The advantages of waterfall PM lie in its rigid structure and predictability, which conversely are disadvantages for certain types of projects.

In the next chapter, you will learn about agile project management, which is a contrasting methodology to waterfall.

[1] https://www.ipma.world/about-us/ipma-international/history-of-ipma/
[2] http://www.ambysoft.com/surveys/success2013.html
[3] https://vitalitychicago.com/blog/agile-projects-are-more-successful-traditional-projects/

READY
SET
AGILE!

CHAPTER 3

AGILE: TWENTY-FIRST CENTURY PROJECT MANAGEMENT

IN the last chapter, we discussed the first type of project management, in which the project occurs in clearly defined stages, and one phase must be completed before the next can begin. However, not all projects are suited for this type of management. Software, especially, requires testing during the entire process rather than leaving it to the end. For some projects, the end goal may not be known at inception. It may require user feedback during the development rather than after the product has been delivered.

Agile project management (APM) offers a more flexible approach. Testing and feedback are intentionally incorporated into the process along the way. Clients also provide comments throughout all stages of management–not just during the requirements and design phases.

Large projects can be broken down into smaller, easy-to-tackle pieces; these steps don't necessarily have to be completed chronologically. The team can work in sprints (or iterations) instead of one long cycle. Because testing occurs continuously, the risk of failure on the project is much lower. Since software fits well in APM, you might not be surprised to find that 71% of agile projects are in the information technology (IT) industry (Nielson, 2013).[4]

Agile Project Management Principles

As you might have guessed from the name, APM is more flexible in its approach. Rather than designing the entire project and disallowing any changes or iterations, with agile, you can incorporate feedback in real time. Due to its flexibility, project managers can get their products to market faster and more efficiently.

Agile projects are also the choice of leading companies, from start-ups all the way to Fortune 500 companies. Projects are characterized by many unknowns. As a project manager, you'll need to be strategizing continuously. With APM, you can adapt to and modify changes on the ground whenever they occur.

Agile project management, rather than being based on a series of discrete stages, is allied to a set of four core values. In chapter eight, I'll introduce you to the 12 principles of the Agile Manifesto. The manifesto flows from these four values, which are integral to any agile project.

1. People and Communication

The agile project is about the people involved and their interactions. There's less importance placed on the tools or the specific processes being used.

2. Working Prototypes

In this type of methodology, the team builds something right away rather than waiting to deliver the final product at the end. In this way,

they can test and find the errors quickly. Clients who might not be entirely sure what they need can quickly find out if what the team is building is the solution they need, or whether there's another iteration necessary.

If the prototype isn't exactly what the client wants, there's no need to go back to the beginning. The entire project doesn't need an overhaul when this happens in agile because the team can simply tweak or rebuild the prototype and continue on their journey. Changes like this don't automatically result in cost overruns or schedule problems, as the need for iterating is built right into the process.

The prototype would take the place of the comprehensive documentation that you would find in a waterfall project. Although it's essential to take notes, it's more important to build something that can then be tested and improved.

3. Stakeholder Collaboration

All stakeholders are invited to give feedback and respond to the prototypes rather than rely only on a project sponsor or the persuasive abilities of a project manager. Communication and collaboration are vital.

When all stakeholders have "skin in the game," they're more invested in the success of the project. They're more willing to remove institutional obstacles and do whatever work they need to do to support the project.

4. Responsiveness to Change

Adaptability and flexibility are crucial to a successful APM project. Our world is rapidly changing. The environment for any project is dynamic, and being responsive to these changes increases the opportunity for project success. Using a rigid structure when the project is in a constant state of flux is a recipe for failure.

It's pretty similar to football plays on the field, as each team must adapt to the conditions on the ground. If a play won't work because the opposing team did something you weren't expecting, there's no reason to continue the play. Do something else that takes advantage of whatever opportunity the other team provided to you.

Phases of a Cycle

Each iteration is like a small cycle. In waterfall PM, there's one long product cycle that can take months to complete. However, in agile, an iteration or sprint lasts about a month. The four steps of each phase are similar to waterfall: requirements, design, implementation, verify (check and deliver). The product then goes into the next monthly sprint or iteration, taking the prototype from the previous iteration and building on that.

During this time, the client (and other stakeholders) all have visibility into the process. The big batches of work are divided into smaller pieces that bring value to clients. These small, actionable deliverables are released to the market without waiting for the entire project to be completed.

Later in the book, you'll discover different agile frameworks such as Scrum and Kanban. No matter the framework, agile projects follow the same six-step process. You may be surprised to learn that so much of the agile process is about planning! The plans described here create the loose structure within which all the flexibility and adaptability fit. For a project to be successful, certain milestones and deliverables must be known or developed ahead of time.

The first three steps are performed at the initial phase of the project and are revised when changes during project execution are incorporated. The last three steps are conducted for every iteration.

1. Planning the Project

What is the end goal, and what does the client need? What's the value to them for a successful completion of the project?

While you can develop the project scope during this phase, it's not set in stone. Client feedback and issues that occur may change the scope at any time and more than once during the project.

2. Roadmap

This is where the team creates the individual features that will eventually make it into the end product. Because these features are built during each iteration, you do need to ensure that these are well planned.

All the features and deliverables make up the product backlog. Team members pull from this and create tasks during later sprints.

3. Stage Planning (Release Planning)

This is the high-level calendar for what features will be released at the end of each cycle. It's known as release planning in the software development world.

4. Sprint Planning

What happens during each iteration? Who works on what? Ensure that the tasks are distributed evenly throughout the sprint. Document the workflow (preferably visually) for the iteration, so team members can understand how the work flows between them. You can also use it to figure out where the bottlenecks occur.

5. Daily Meetings

These should take no more than 15 minutes each morning. Each member should discuss what they did the day before and what they have left to work on for that day. This isn't a planning session or problem-solving session, but a time to keep everyone in the loop in terms of how the workflow is being satisfied.

6. Review

At the end of the sprint, you would first hold a review with the stakeholders so they can see the finished sprint product (feature release in software). Secondly, you would need to have a retrospective with them: what went well, what didn't, and what might require improvement.

Accurate and relevant metrics for planning and performance measurements are more than just how the project is tracking against schedule and cost, which is done in waterfall. Agile focuses on providing results, improving performance, and adopting data-driven decisions. Performance metrics include:

- **Cycle time:** How much time is spent working on a given process item.
- **Lead time:** How long it takes from the client's request to the delivery of the item.
- **Aging work in progress:** How much work is not being done, or "aging."
- **Throughput:** How much work is completed compared to the time used.

Agile focuses on forecasting as opposed to "gut feelings" when it comes to scheduling and planning a project. A forecast requires data from previous experiences that provide an estimate for how long a step will take and how much it may cost. Every project is different, so the forecast won't be 100% accurate. However, you'll be able to give your clients more realistic expectations regarding your project delivery.

The Primary Focus of APM

As you may recall from the last chapter, the reason for waterfall project management is the *deliverable*–that is, whatever the client has requested and the project team agreed to hand over. It's about the bridge or the building being built, not the construction company or real estate developer. The focus should be clear, and everyone involved in a waterfall project should know what the outcome of the project will be.

Agile projects are concerned with the people involved, not the documentation or process. Of course, there's specific documentation on agile projects, and also processes to be followed (the four-step iteration cycle, as described earlier). However, that's not where the focus of the project lies; such is on the collaboration and interaction with *stakeholders*, which is where APM shines.

Roles and Skills Required

Even though there's no top-down cascade of the process like there is in waterfall, teams still need a project manager with the same responsibilities as one conducting a waterfall project. The skills are the same (though an agile project manager may need to be even better at communication than a traditional one).

Due to the flexible nature of agile, team members must be adaptable and curious about the project and its environs. They also must have a bit of an entrepreneurial mindset, because APM doesn't always tell team members what to do at all times. On occasions, they'll need to figure it out for themselves, especially when something changes.

McKinsey recommends a variety of team members with diverse expertise (Brocchi et al., 2016).[5] You will need developers in a software project, in addition to an integration lead who can help ensure that all layers of the software work together.

No matter the industry, there should be a **product owner** who ties the development in with user feedback. This requires a **tech lead** to make sure the product's built correctly, and a **business system lead** who makes sure the product still fits with the business use case. All projects need at least one **subject-matter expert** in the industry, as well as a **Quality Assurance leader**.

Advantages of APM

As you've seen in this chapter, agile is based on flexibility and the capacity for change. It's best for projects that take advantage of this, which is why it's most commonly used in the IT industry, especially software. However, many different companies, including those in the Fortune 500, are adopting agile as well (Hisock, 2016).[6] In addition to software, firms are beginning to use the methodology for their customer service, sales, and marketing efforts.

- **Higher client satisfaction**

  There are no surprises in APM because the customer has visibility into the entire process. An agile team doesn't show up after months of hard work with a product that the client didn't know they were getting, which can happen with a waterfall project.

  In addition, the very process of APM rests on focusing on the client. The client would remain involved and engaged in every step of the way. Their wishlist is prioritized, so the features that are most important to them can be released more quickly.

- **Increased product quality**

  Unlike a more traditional PM process, agile doesn't leave the quality assurance to the very end. There's no need to rush through it to make the deadline. Quality is tested as the monthly sprint occurs, so any faults can be found—and fixed—fast.

Besides, APM encompasses a review and retrospective at the end of the sprint. At the end of each phase, the team asks themselves (and the client): what went well? What could have gone better? What can we improve? This allows for lessons to be learned quickly in time for the next sprint. They also won't be left to the very end of the project, only to be used on the next one.

- **Faster ROI**

Prototypes are created and tested rapidly, which means the product or service can be brought to the market more quickly. The earlier to market, the faster the company can profit.

A months-long development timeline doesn't work for companies in rapidly changing environments, such as IT. Being able to adapt quickly to customers' changing tastes and requirements gives the company an edge on their competition.

- **Reduced Risks**

APM is much less likely to fail because the deliverable is continuously tested for quality. If something happens in the broader environment, it's easier to switch to the "new normal," as we've found during the time of the coronavirus.

The client is less likely to be surprised by the ultimate product, the time frame, or the budget because they were involved in the entire process.

Shorter cycles also mean that failure is discovered quickly rather than after months of work. If it fails, the team can tweak and start again. In a waterfall project, the entire thing might need to be scrapped, or all that work has to start again with another timeline and with another budget. In agile, changes aren't very costly, and the possibility of change is built right into the phase structure.

- **Better project control**

  Daily sprint meetings allow the project manager to know if everyone is on time and budget. Clients benefit from transparency and can intervene if necessary.

- **Better human resource management**

  Each team member is always working on the most up-to-date version of their tasks. There's little to no time wasting since one person doesn't need the other to finish before they begin.

Disadvantages of APM

- **Limited documentation**

  Although some documentation is produced for an agile project, it's not as comprehensive as it is for a waterfall. Project managers or team members seeking to reproduce a portion of a previous iteration may not have the tools they need to do so. In other words, they often need to reinvent the wheel when looking back at an earlier phase.

- **Suboptimal resource planning**

  Because the entire project isn't planned in advance, new materials or services—or even team members—may be required for a later iteration. They won't be in the original timeline or budget.

  Being unable to produce a list of necessities for the procurement department ahead of time means they may be unable to take advantage of bulk pricing as they would for a more linear project.

- **No clear end**

  A waterfall project has a clearly defined finished product. Because an agile one has a number of iterations, it's not always clear what the finished product should actually be. Some projects can iterate almost indefinitely.

- **Scope creep**

  As iterations go by, the team may discover new functionalities or opportunities that lead to new features. The more this happens, the farther away the end of the project becomes, which increases the need for resources, both material and human.

- **Harder to measure**

  With no clear way to measure whether a project is on schedule or not, it's also difficult to know which metrics apply for any given phase. Progress doesn't happen one step at a time as it does for a waterfall project; it occurs over several iterations, which makes it harder to track.

- **More time spent on non-project tasks**

  APM requires a lot of communication among team members and between the team and its client(s). The team spends a lot of time connecting with others and coordinating, as opposed to having task-specific activities.

Key Takeaways

Agile project management isn't without disadvantages, but it fits better with many projects in the modern world that require the ability to adapt and ensure the clients are on board with all necessary adjustments.

- Agile project management is based on the four core values of people, working prototype, stakeholder collaboration, and responsiveness to change.
- There are six phases of an APM project, three of which occur at the beginning: overall planning, roadmap creation, and release plan; and three of which occur during the month-long sprints: sprint planning, daily meetings, and review.
- The key focus of an agile project is on the client, as opposed to the deliverable focus of a waterfall project.
- Team members and the project manager on an agile project must be flexible and able to change with the situation.
- The key advantages of APM aren't just for software developers, and they revolve around its flexibility and adaptability. The disadvantages are the flip side of the benefits.

In the next chapter, you will learn about agile project management software, and whether it can be incorporated into your personal life as well.

[4] https://dzone.com/articles/growing-agile-how-popular

[5] https://www.mckinsey.com/business-functions/mckinsey-digital/our-insights/using-agile-to-accelerate-your-data-transformation

[6] https://www.business2community.com/business-innovation/fortune-500-companies-transform-agile-buzzword-business-model-01625695

READY
SET
AGILE!

CHAPTER 4

STOP, COLLABORATE, AND LISTEN: APM SOFTWARE

CURRENTLY, there are a variety of software solutions that automate tools, such as Gantt charts, spreadsheets, and mind maps. The more manual entry is required, the more chance there is for human error to enter the equation. Automation also makes the work more transparent since anyone can access these tools. An effective project manager would hire the best people for their ability to think and create—not their data entry skills. These people would be hired for their professional work and not their ability to spend time on complicated or manual applications.

These applications are easy-to-use, even for those who are not so great with technology. They all have user-friendly interfaces, allowing you to jump in and start working immediately and intuitively. You'll find they're more efficient than spreadsheets and notepads. Once you've begun to tap into their functionality, you'll be amazed by how much routine work you no longer have to perform and how much time you free up for thinking and developing.

Using project management software will allow you to choose templates or files that you may have previously applied in other successful projects. Once you change something on a project, it will flow through to all the other tasks, as appropriate. Most of these tools provide graphics—they're more natural for the brain to process than walls of text while highlighting any necessary information. All of which makes it easier for the entire team to track progress and understand where they are in the cycle. Automated notifications mean that no one has to rely on remembering to send a task to the next person or get started on a task that was assigned a few weeks ago.

Comparing PM Software Applications

Let's start with the traditional software before we move on to what's available with agile. There's less need for some of the flexibility and collaboration activities in a traditional project, so the software commonly used for these projects won't have the same functionality.

For example, one software for use with a waterfall project is Project Manager ("Waterfall Methodology," n.d.).[7] It allows you to automate the Gantt chart, which is one of the essential tools for a waterfall manager. With the software, you can reduce the number of manual entries required, making a Gantt chart using a spreadsheet tool. It provides online document storage as well, which comes in handy for the extensive documentation requirements of a traditional project. Also, you can develop a dashboard that shows your progress, budget vs. actual expenses, and the team's workload, or you can create templates for concepts that you'll use again later. Traditional PM software may also include customizable calendars, which are important for projects that are timeline-dependent.

By contrast, software designed for APM requires additional functionality. Though Gantt charts may be included, they're not as important. The ideal software must provide the ability to collaborate without relying on email threads that quickly become long and harder to follow. They'll also include time tracking capabilities, so each member will know if they're staying on track and budget. Tasks can be assigned to more than one team member where necessary. Whoever requires visibility on a task can have it, as long as they're a user on the project. Everything that's needed for successful project completion is located in one place.

This type of software helps teams to estimate costs and use visualization to show progress. It's much easier to spot any bottlenecks that might be occurring with a visual tool. They also include workflow management features that permit the allocation of duties among team members.

When dealing with iterative projects, especially in software development, your team will find issues. They must be tracked, and most APM software comes with the ability to spot and follow them.

Though APM software has additional features, it's designed primarily to avoid overwhelming those who have a harder time with technology. You don't need to know that much about project management or how it works to use these tools. Though each application has its advantages and disadvantages, most of them will work equally well for most agile project managers and their teams. The interfaces are intuitive, so you can get to work quickly.

An agile project is designed to focus on the client, and help project teams achieve those goals. It's not about mastering a piece of technology; it's about recognizing what the client wants and using the software as a tool to automate the management process easily. Less time dealing with manual tasks allows for more time to think and analyze.

Best Features of Commonly Used APM Software

Although there are plenty of software tools available, most teams use one of the following for their needs. If you're on a team that's already using one of these tools, you'll get along fine by using their existing software. However, if you're starting new, your project may fit better with one than another, given their key benefits.

- **Asana**

  Asana gathers all objectives, tasks, priorities, and responsibilities in one place. You can monitor the team and its progress in real-time, and it contains an audit trail along with workflow and task management for bugs. You'll find process mapping and everything you need for collaboration–including brainstorming, discussion boards, contact management, and version control–within this software.

  Productivity benefits include team chat and file sharing, plus all the project tracking tools such as Gantt charts (if you use them), time tracking, milestone tracking, prioritization, percent-complete tracking, and a view of any to-do lists created.

  Because it has many different features available, Asana is suitable for a variety of projects and teams.

- **Trello**

  The same company owns this software and JIRA (in the next section). Trello is designed to be a visual collaboration tool, with benefits including business management features, such as inventory and order management, as well as scheduling. You can create product roadmaps and use other product management devices like idea management, prioritization, and milestone tracking.

Trello's remote support features, such as employee activity monitoring, live chat, and remote access, allow employees all over the globe to stay connected.

- **JIRA**

This is the application most used by agile software development teams, based on over a decade of agile evolution, and is continuously updated ("JIRA," n.d.).[8] It's helpful for teams that need to iterate and release faster. There are fewer collaboration tools than in some of the other software tools mentioned here, but it allows team members to track issues and supports both marketing teams and IT developers.

All product management tools are enabled, including prioritization, release management, road mapping, and workflow management. It's helpful for those who require project portfolio management (PPM), which is the centralized management for multiple projects and analyzes results to be implemented in other projects.

- **Basecamp**

Do you want to bring all the tasks and necessary tools together? This software allows users to collaborate with discussion boards, document management, and calendar management. It also provides remote access for its users. Teams that would like to increase communication will find Basecamp beneficial, as it contains news feeds, real-time chats, discussion threads, alerts, and notifications. Users may find it easy to use because its interface resembles many common social media platforms.

- **ClickUp**

This software technology is excellent for those wanting their goals, time tracking, scheduling, calendar, and inbox to be all in one place. It's a rich resource for collaboration, and also includes all kinds of Gantt chart applications. Its productivity and project management tools are comprehensive, including project planning as well.

ClickUp contains resource management benefits, such as capacity management, resource allocation, and even skills tracking. Time tracking is another key feature of the software.

Like Asana, it has a breadth of features that make it suitable for a variety of projects.

Tips for Selecting the Best Project Management Tools

Basic tools as simple as post-it notes and whiteboards are considered project management tools since you can adopt them in the management and execution of your project. However, automation enables your team to do more thinking and decision-making and less manual work. You want software tools to automate routine tasks, so you and the team are freed up to do the important work.

Agile core values are included within the project management tools discussed earlier in the chapter, so whichever one you choose will work for your agile project. However, depending on the focus of your project, one program may be a better fit than another. The pricing also differs somewhat among the various tools, so what would work for a smaller team might be cost-prohibitive on a larger team.

Here are a few questions you should answer before deciding on which agile project management tools are most suitable for your team:

1. How many projects do you expect to be managing at any given time?

2. What is the size of your team, and how many people will need the software?

3. Does it have the potential for growth alongside your organization?

4. Is it user-friendly, even for team members who aren't so great with technology? Asking people who have used the software in the past, as well as consulting user reviews, will give you some idea of how intuitive each interface is.

5. Does it support remote work? Many people expect that, after we're no longer social distancing due to the coronavirus, that fewer people will be working on location (Lazarow, 2020).[9] Also, it is common for teams to be spread around across different countries and time zones.

6. Will you need to integrate your software with other tools? If you already have some enterprise resource planning tools in your organization, be sure they're compatible.

APM Software is Not Just for "Official" Work Projects

As we've mentioned before, everyone manages projects in their personal life or the workplace, even if it isn't officially designated as a project. Suppose you need to put together a presentation—wouldn't it be more efficient to create all the tasks that need to be done in the project software, along with the timelines? For example, you will need to write the script, build the slides, find the graphics and supporting documents, and rehearse it, all by a specific deadline. You may also require subtasks, such as obtaining quotes from senior management and inserting videos.

If you entered it all in your software, you'd receive notifications to start a new task, and you'd be able to track your progress quickly. If you were partnering with a colleague or two, you can divide and assign the tasks too. You'd have a chat or discussion board where everyone could log in and ask questions or make status reports. Yes, you'd need to spend a bit of time entering everything in, but after that, everything has been tracked and automated.

Likewise, you might have some personal projects that software can make considerably easier. Suppose you're moving cross-country—I've done it three times and let me tell you, there's a lot of logistics involved! Rather than scribbling out the extensive list of tasks that must be accomplished before the movers even step foot in your house, or entering that data into a spreadsheet where it's difficult to prioritize, you can use a PM software.

Automated reminders are beneficial because, with big projects, there will be something that you've forgotten! Many tasks are dependent on one another. For example, you will need to clear out the garage before you take what you don't want to the dump or the donation store. However, these tasks can occur at the same time that you're getting quotes from moving companies and choosing one to work with. If you're married, you and your spouse can divide the tasks between yourselves and work on them separately. You'll both have access to the timeline that shows whether you're on schedule or not.

APM Software Is Useful for Optimizing Whatever You're Working On

Even smaller projects might benefit from using the software, with its automatic reminders and progress chart. Software is a tool to make your life more efficient and productive. The time you save entering

task reminders manually or checking off completed tasks is time you could focus on real, important tasks with added value.

Once you become used to the software, you will find many uses for it outside your employment. All software, no matter what kind it is or what it's used for, does have at least a little bit of a learning curve while first learning how it works. However, once you're past that curve, it's pretty simple to spot projects that could benefit from the project management tool you're already using.

The basics of APM software are pretty similar, no matter which one you're using. You'll find that, for most projects, whichever one you're familiar with will work perfectly fine. If your company has adopted one of the tools listed above, it will work for most of your projects.

In other words, don't spend too much time agonizing over which one to pick if you're starting from scratch! Any of these software tools will provide you with the fundamental functionality you're looking for on your projects. Some may have more features than others, and some will be more suited for specific types of projects than others. Nevertheless, the underlying benefits will support any project manager and their team.

Key Takeaways

Project management software helps people do their work more efficiently by automating tasks that are of low value or which require too much input when done manually. They encourage team cooperation, as well.

- Agile project management software requires more functionality than software for traditional projects, but they are very intuitive and easy to learn.
- APM software applications have standard features that are necessary for any agile project, and some will be more suitable for specific projects and goals.
- Ask yourself several questions about what may fit your projects and work style best when choosing software.
- You can use agile software for other projects too, both at work and home.
- No matter which software tool you choose, it will help you manage whatever projects you're currently working on.

In the next chapter, we will unveil the Ready, Set, Agile methodology.

[7] https://www.projectmanager.com/software/use-cases/waterfall-methodology
[8] https://www.capterra.com/p/19319/JIRA/
[9] https://www.marketwatch.com/story/why-you-may-still-be-working-from-home-after-the-coronavirus-crisis-is-over-2020-03-26

READY
SET
AGILE!

CHAPTER

READY, SET, AGILE!

HOW exactly do you plan an Agile project from start to finish? Remember when you were a little kid running a race or swimming, and an adult would shout, *Ready, set, GO!* That was the signal to get going. It may seem pretty simplistic, but it's an easy way to think about planning a project.

A traditional project is planned from start to finish, and no work is commenced until the detailed planning is complete. However, in an Agile environment, some planning will happen upfront, whereas some will occur later during the sprint. Planning is the **"Ready"** section of Ready, Set, Agile.

Closely following the ready stage is **"Set,"** which consists of short team meetings, including those with the client.

The **"Agile"** stage is when the work is performed. This would be the execution of the plans made during Ready, and fine-tuned during Set.

There are at least two Ready, Set, Agile components to every project; there is one for the overall project, where the framework for the whole project is determined. Because of the flexible nature of APM, this first component will only provide the skeleton or structure for the project. The second component would be during each monthly sprint. There's a bit of planning for that specific sprint in the Ready stage, daily meetings that occur during Set, and the execution of the sprint in Agile.

I created the Ready, Set, Agile framework to help me during each phase and task. I often got overloaded and trapped in details—I'd lose the main objective and lead meetings in the wrong direction. For these reasons, I found it very helpful to use a mind map or other easy-to-remember structure. Nevertheless, I then said to myself, *wait a second!* What is the overall objective of this activity? What stage am I in? Once I know where I am, I can perform the right step to get me toward my goal. Otherwise, if I take the wrong step, I set myself up for failure. Am I doing the right things and communicating in accordance with this goal instead of my current preference?

I like sports. Men and women train hard to be Ready for a competition. Before the race or match, they would warm up, plan their tactics, and get on their marks to Set before they go. At the go moment, those who prepared best would be most *agile* and, eventually, would win the race.

Project management is very similar to sports. If you perform all the prep and meetings correctly, all team members will become more effective, and you will achieve your goals more efficiently. Projects, like sports seasons, can last for months, and obstacles and defeats do happen. However, endurance and doing the right things correctly can create a winning team.

I hope my Ready, Set, Agile framework will serve you well. However, as we all have different preferences, you may find your own way to memorize and name the necessary activities. Feel free to apply what suits you best.

Overall Project: Ready (Planning)

The first stage of any project is the initiation stage, where the project and its objectives are established. This would be where you determine the scope, budget, and timeline for the entire project. You'll need to estimate the resources required, considering labor, materials, and equipment. The clients will provide feedback and the outcome they're looking for during this stage.

With agile project management, everyone involved in the project is aware that things will change over time and as circumstances require. Therefore, the plan at the outset of a project would be more like a framework–it's the skeleton of the plan, and the details about functions and designs will be developed later during the monthly sprints.

Another way to think about the Ready stage of the project is by comparing it to football. This is your training camp time, where you're building your strategy. You won't know exactly how you'll defeat your opponents several months from now, and your team may not have its precise game plan yet because that specific plan depends on the games your and their team will be playing between now and then. You're laying the groundwork for those wins during this time.

Planning includes identifying the key stakeholders of the project. In addition to the requirements that you've discussed with the clients and the resource estimation that you've completed for the plan, there are two more steps in the Ready phase at the outset of the project.

1. Product Roadmap

This enables you to design which features will be developed along the way for the final product. Each one will be the result of a monthly sprint, and (ideally) they will build on each other until you reach the ultimate deliverable.

For instance, suppose you're working on a project for a new type of car. The product roadmap would describe the features of the engine, the body, and so on. With every sprint–or stage in the construction of the car–your team would add an additional piece until the new car is fully developed.

Another component of the product roadmap is the **product backlog**. It captures the features, deliverables, and requirements for each monthly sprint. At the beginning of each sprint, the team would merely refer to the product backlog and pull tasks and requirements from there.

2. Stage (Release) Planning

Traditional waterfall project teams have just one implementation date after the entire project has been developed. Agile projects break down their project development into shorter cycles, and new features are released at the end of each cycle or sprint.

Stage planning (known as release planning for IT developers) provides a clear-cut knowledge of the feature release for every sprint. You would include its quality assurance and targets here, to the extent that they're known.

For example, suppose you're on a team that's developing a mobile app. One sprint might be to discover the needs and desires of your ideal users. The release for this sprint would be knowing your ideal client and their needs. The next sprint might be developing a solution for those needs. Then, the final sprint would be coding the solution to be released on the mobile platform. This particular example would last only three months, but some projects could easily take much longer. The number of sprints needed will depend on the complexity of the project; therefore, the length from the planning stage to the final product would also vary according to the complexity.

Overall Project: Set (Meetings)

Critical values of APM are the focus on people and communications, so meetings are essential. Agile is predicated on flexibility and adaptation. Since changes can spring up quickly, meetings help everyone adjust to whatever new direction may be necessary.

During the initial stage, there's only one meeting that counts: the project kickoff, which sets the tone for the rest of the work. The client and team come together to understand the nature of the entire project and how it will work, including a summary of the roadmap and the stage or release plans.

The team and client will understand the overall goal of the project, the deliverables, and the estimated timeframe. Everything completed in the planning (Ready) section would be communicated throughout. You'll establish metrics, so both the client and team know how progress is measured.

Overall Project: Agile (Execution)

Now, you're finally ready to sprint! Most of the execution takes place during the sprints, but from the initial kickoff, the team is ready to get moving. Think of hitting the field during the football game; the team is now getting ready to start making the plays.

In this stage, you would monitor how the whole project develops. That would include whether current sprints are being completed on time, and if customer requirements are being incorporated and communicated well. You are completing the current sprint, upcoming sprints are nearing, and you are starting the planning—who from the team would play a key role and what needs to be done in advance. Use a bird's eye view on the execution to see how everything fits.

Sprint: Ready (Planning)

For each sprint, you should know from the overall plan what you're trying to accomplish. Now you need to plan your sprint. Who works on which task in this phase? Team members should perform specific tasks based on their strengths.

How long should each task take? The workload should be distributed as evenly as possible to ensure that the timeline is met, and the feature meant to be released during this sprint is completed and quality tested by the end of the month. The product owner and team would also meet to discuss the product backlog.

If you were on a football team, this would be where you'd develop the strategy for the team you're playing this week. You would have watched the footage and drawn conclusions about the best way to defeat them. You will also want to get specific about how your team has been playing and how it matches up against the other team.

Sprint: Set (Meetings)

Communication is key! There will be daily meetings during the sprint, meant to be stand-up only and completed in fifteen minutes or so. Each team member would discuss what they got done the previous day and what they expect to achieve that day. The aim of these meetings is not to have an elaborate discussion of new items, but just as a way to keep every member of the team accountable to the rest of the team members and everyone informed. In football terms, this is the huddle before the play or during a time out. The team would agree on the specific tactics they plan to use for the play.

There are also meetings at the end of each sprint, in which the team and the client would review what went well and what could be improved for next time. This part would be similar to when a football team reviews the game.

Sprint: Agile (Execute)

All the tasks in the sprint, discussed in the planning and meetings, are executed during this phase of the sprint. Here's where the work gets done—the prototype is developed and quality tested before the end of the month when the feature is intended for release.

This is where the ability to track progress in the software and visualize the project status is so important. Something that happens during a sprint may affect the next sprint after that one. The flexibility to adapt to changes is vital during the execution phase. If something goes wrong, the team will need to either fix or scrap it and start again. Team members need to keep an eye on their budget (for both time and money) as they work and communicate if they're off, so the rest of the team can adjust. The original release that was planned for the sprint may need to change or be tweaked during the process as well.

When you're thinking of football, agile would be equivalent to the play; that would be the quarterback passing to the receiver or trying to move the ball a few yards down the field. In other words, it is whatever can be done in the time available! The plan may have been originally to throw to one of the receivers, but if they're not open, the quarterback needs to adjust and pass to another, or run the ball instead.

Team Collaboration Tips

When it comes to projects, you must all work as one team. There is a need for every member to make it function as a cohesive unit. Every member has work to complete, and all must communicate with each other and the client to ensure that the project is successful—just as all football players on the field have to work together to win. Here are a few tips to boost collaboration in a team setting.

- **Learn about one another**

  Team members need to feel free to socialize and interact with one another. It doesn't all have to be "shop talk." Teams that work well together often meet outside the project for lunch or other hang out and team bonding activities.

- **Embrace personality differences**

  People learn and communicate differently because they're all from various cultures and backgrounds. Encourage the team to learn about each other's preferences and how to live with them.

  Having a variety of experiences and feeling comfortable to open up about them will actually make the team stronger because it allows the members to share ideas freely. When everyone is more alike than not, it's common to fall into "groupthink," where no one will want to be different from everyone else, thus unable to share new ideas. Groupthink also causes people to want to avoid responsibility for making decisions; since everyone agrees, no one can be blamed.

- **Provide a quick recap at the end of a meeting**

  Just to be sure that no one is left out on team goals, recap the main points after every team meeting and encourage people to speak up if they are confused about something.

Key Takeaways

Although I created Ready, Set, Agile to make it easy to remember the structure of agile projects, you can choose whatever strategy will make it easy for you to remember.

- APM can be described as Ready, Set, Agile.
- **Ready** is the planning stage, which occurs at the beginning of the project and each monthly sprint.
- **Set** is in the form of meetings–a project kickoff at the beginning and daily team meetings, as well as the review and retrospective at the end of the sprint.
- **Agile** is the execution of all project work.
- To have a winning team, encourage them to get to know each other and celebrate their differences.

In the next chapter, you will learn about the Scrum framework.

CHAPTER 6

LET'S START THE MATCH: SCRUM FRAMEWORK

IN rugby, the scrum (short for "scrimmage") starts a match. A rugby scrum requires eight players from each team to huddle up in three rows, with the goal being to grab the ball. Similarly, the purpose of the Scrum method of project management is to work together as a team to accomplish the objective.

Why Scrum Is So Popular

This is the most popular Agile methodology (Townsend, 2013).[10] It is so widely spread that, for some people, Scrum is the only agile model they know.

It's a simple way to implement APM because there's a structure that's ready for team members to use. The framework makes it a little more familiar for those who are used to traditional project management; thus, it helps them ease into an Agile environment. Later in the book, we'll discuss the Agile Manifesto, but teams don't necessarily need to be familiar with it to use Scrum.

Scrum doesn't provide a paint-by-number, step-by-step method for any given project. The team would decide the tools and materials they prefer to use, and the process control for Scrum isn't a top-down approach (as usually seen in a traditional project). It's empirical, meaning it's based on what the team observes as it moves through the process. This makes Scrum highly adaptive in complex and ever-changing situations.

Scrum is defined by its meetings and roles, some of which are familiar to waterfall project teams. There are certifications available to those who want to master Scrum, which we'll discuss in detail later. Those who are moving from a command-and-control system into a flexible and self-organizing agile methodology find Scrum as a suitable framework. It can be used for projects of any size, though it fits more complex projects very well. Although it is most often used in IT, many industries have adopted the Scrum framework, including human resources, education, and marketing.

Scrum helps the organization discover what works best for it without imposing restrictions or constraints.

How It Works Within Agile

You will find the whole Ready, Set, Agile framework we described in the previous chapter is present in a Scrum project. The client and team would create an overall plan at the beginning, and the execution takes place in monthly sprints. Each sprint is planned in more detail at the beginning, known as **sprint planning**. There are daily meetings during the sprint, which may be referred to as **Scrum**

meetings or stand-ups because the intent is to keep it so short that everyone can stand up for the whole thing. There's a **review meeting** at the end of each sprint to discuss what went well and what didn't. A feature is released at the end of every sprint that builds up to the final product or service.

The Scrum framework admits that the team members and stakeholders don't know everything about the project ahead of time. Learning must be incorporated into the project during the sprints—not developed at the very end of the process. It takes some time to master Scrum because you'll need to use it consistently while familiarizing yourself with the process. The more you use it, the easier it will be, and using the Scrum methodology continually will help you improve.

In chapter three, we introduced the four core values of agile. Scrum builds on these values and is governed by the following **three pillars**:

- **Transparency**

  Everyone, including team members and stakeholders, understands the goals of the project, as well as their individual roles and responsibilities. A common language is used, especially for the processes.

  When is the project "done?" There's a single definition that everyone is clear about. They all attend the daily meetings and have clarity on the tools in use.

- **Inspection**

  The crucial aspect of inspection is that it's not just performed by someone assigned to the QA aspect of the project. Everyone involved looks for faults or variances and corrects them. Inspection isn't only about the product—people and processes undergo it as well.

- **Adaptation**

  The team adapts with transparent inspection and workflows as needed. The review meeting that occurs at the end of every sprint is vital because the client and team can agree on things that require improvement, which can be implemented immediately in the next sprint.

In addition to the three pillars, Scrum is also guided by the **five core values**. A successful Scrum team learns to integrate them into everything they do.

- **Commitment**

  In a command-and-control structure present in a traditional PM background, commitment has a slightly different meaning. It's the expectation that the scope of the project is fulfilled, no matter what. In Scrum, commitment is applied to your actions. Team members who are committed dedicate themselves to the process.

  Scrum members commit to the sprint goal, values, three pillars, learning, and improving. The end result may look quite different because Scrum is adapting as the circumstances and clients require.

- **Focus**

  You don't have to be a Zen master at focusing on the now–you just need to be on a Scrum project. You know that you'll make changes as necessary and adapt, so there's no point in worrying about what might be coming down the road. There's only a need to focus on that which is being done right now.

  What is the simplest thing that might work now? What can we learn from the current project and use it in the future?

- **Openness**

  This quality is necessary for anyone who needs to adapt to change. However, in Scrum, it's not just an openness to new circumstances; it's an openness to team members who don't think, act, or work alike, and a willingness to accept feedback, both positive and negative, to improve. It is also the ability to work with stakeholders, no matter what their concerns may be.

- **Respect**

  The only way to collaborate well as a team is for all the members to respect one another. Diversity in ideas and background, as noted earlier, makes the team stronger. Team members can learn new things when they're exposed to new opinions and experiences. Clients appreciate respect, as well!

  Team members respect users by providing solutions, but also by not wasting time on features that are not necessary or won't be used. They respect the Scrum framework and the associated roles and responsibilities.

- **Courage**

  You may be wondering why a project management team needs courage! It does take some bravery to admit that requirements and people aren't perfect, and also to be transparent with people you may not know or aren't very familiar with. It takes courage to change direction in the middle of a project because the environment requires it.

In addition to the core values and pillars, there's some additional terminology that goes along with the Scrum methodology. You'll find several terms you're already familiar with from the general discussion of agile.

A **product backlog** is a list of all requirements, features, and bug fixes to deliver with the product. Every time a new sprint starts, the product backlog would guide the team toward what needs to be accomplished. It's similar to the Work Breakdown Structure (WBS) in traditional PM, but isn't completed at the beginning of the project and is linear rather than with a tree structure. It's consistently updated as requirements evolve. Although it exists in agile, it is given a more prominent role in a Scrum project. There's one person in charge of it who would organize, groom, and update it, known as the product owner.

The **sprint backlog** consists of the tasks chosen from the product backlog to help the team meet the sprint goal, which is the deliverable at the end of the sprint.

Also, in Scrum as in agile, the work is conducted in sprints, and the work for each sprint is planned out at the beginning of the sprint itself (sprint planning). Whatever's being undertaken during the current sprint is known as the sprint backlog. The daily meeting is known as a Scrum meeting, but the function is the same.

What's new in Scrum is the concept of the **Scrum board**. Most software packages dedicated to agile offer this option, but some teams prefer to use a whiteboard and dry erase markers for the purpose. It helps the team keep track of the current sprint visually. The board is divided simply into three sections: To-Do, In Progress, and Done. Tasks are moved around as appropriate.

Another tool used in Scrum that may also be included in the software is the **burndown chart**. It shows what progress has been made on the sprint goal and how much more is left to go. Ideally, the remainder to be done "burns down" to zero by the end of the sprint.

Remember that Scrum operates on a common language! The team has specific criteria for *Done*, and each item in the product backlog has a list of parameters that specifies when the item is Done.

Another concept unique to Scrum is the **user story**. It explains what each feature is and why it's crucial for the user. It's intended to be short and straightforward, and helps the team members understand why this feature should be prioritized and built. A user story often follows a simple template: "As a <type of user>, I want <the goal> because <reason>" ("User Stories," n.d.).[11]

If you're familiar with the term **increment**, you can probably guess what it means in a Scrum context. It's what has been completed in previous sprints up to the current sprint. Before it can be a product increment, it has to meet the team's definition of Done. This is specified in the sprint backlog.

The other concept that is specific to Scrum is known as the **artifact**. The main three artifacts are the product backlog, sprint backlog, and increment.

Scrum Process

The Scrum process is pretty straightforward and can be described in the following five steps:

1. The product owner creates the product backlog.
2. The product backlog is used in the sprint planning session, where it's broken down into small parts.
3. The team creates a sprint backlog and plans out the sprint, usually one to four weeks in duration.
4. During the execution, the team (and sometimes stakeholders) gather for daily Scrum meetings.
5. At the end of the sprint, after delivery, there's a review meeting.

Best Practices for a Dream Team

If you want to create a high-functioning dream team, it's best to follow these 11 best practices.

- **Peer-to-peer collaboration**

  Software serves tremendously across projects and teams. Members can share in real time and have their questions answered by those who've worked with a similar issue. Having one platform for user stories, task lists, and other artifacts can help all members work on complex projects.

- **Develop transparent artifacts**

  Transparency is one of the three key pillars, and it translates into the artifacts as well. Everyone on the team needs to know what's being built and why. This builds trust among the team and stakeholders.

  When all are involved in the product backlog, for example, the team understands why the customer wants a particular feature. Likewise, the customer can see the estimate of how much work may be involved in generating the end product.

- **Involve stakeholders**

  The team may want to invite certain stakeholders to some of the daily meetings as appropriate, so they can understand what's going on. Their input is invaluable in the user stories, which help clarify the intentions and priorities for the team. They may also be involved in the sprint planning, where they can both contribute and see into the process that will occur.

  Having the stakeholders present for estimation allows the team members to ask questions directly. It also provides

the customer with an understanding of how the team arrived at the estimate.

All this helps build trust between the stakeholders and the team, aiding in managing the client's expectations as well.

- **Continually improve**

  With the repeated iterations that a Scrum team must go through to deliver the product, there is an opportunity to build a better process as it goes along. The peer-to-peer collaboration facilitates this as well. At the end of the sprint, when the team conducts its review and retrospective, there's no reason to let the lessons learned fade into the background; they can and *should* be used to improve continually.

- **Automate and scale Scrum for the enterprise**

  Lessons learned on one Scrum team can be escalated to all the teams working on a project. A Scrum project in one area of the company can be scaled to all the projects enterprise-wide. Documenting and automating the best practices across the organization helps make all teams more efficient.

- **Keep together and build the team**

  Teams that work well together should be kept together wherever possible (if it isn't broke, don't fix it!) Maintaining the same team won't always be possible, as some teams need certain types of experts or roles.

  Involve new team members in team-building activities. This shouldn't be just with team lunches or Scrum games, but more professional events like knowledge-sharing and supporting practices that can promote collaboration.

- **Plan for a six-hour day**

  Most teams work eight-hour days, but you never know when life is going to happen, or otherwise, a spanner gets thrown into the works. A team member may be unable to work during a day. Planning for a six-hour day allows for time to handle unexpected occurrences. As you know, agile and Scrum are all about adaptability, so the team will need some time to deal with unpleasant surprises.

- **Plan the correct amount of work**

  If the product backlog doesn't have enough work for two or more sprints, it may be tempting to let the scope increase. Sprint plan only when the backlog is big enough.

  You won't want to stretch the sprint to achieve the goal when the story is bigger than expected or more stories are coming. Conversely, don't cut the sprint short if the story is completed early. Instead, maintain the sprint end by cutting back on the story or adding a small, new one as appropriate.

- **Use visualizations**

  Our brains understand visual information faster than words. Keep the team and stakeholders aware of progress with clear and visual presentations. Add the user story to the Scrum board to keep track of its progress and maintain the burndown chart to see if completion matches up to plan. You can use a similar chart with all the sprints included comparing actual sprint progress to the plan.

- **Evaluate velocity**

  Comparing actual time to complete a task with the original plan will help the team estimate the duration in the future better. Usually, you should be able to complete 3-5 sprints to get a good measure of velocity ("25 Best Scrum Practices," n.d.).[12] If you still have a lot of variations in sprints after a handful of them, you may need to reconsider your planning. The team needs to be able to spread the stories fairly evenly throughout each sprint.

- **In software development, resolve bugs next sprint**

  It's one of the best practices to fix all bugs in one sprint that follows their identification. That way, you're not dealing with a huge list of bugs as you near the end of the process. Trying to fix them immediately in the current sprint usually throws off your schedule. Plan for them in the upcoming sprint instead.

Scrum Roles

Traditional project management is more in command-and-control mode, delivering their instructions top down. One person usually fulfills the project manager role. They must not only understand the product and the client (product owner) but also encourage and build the team (Scrum master). There may not be a project manager on a Scrum project; by contrast, the Scrum roles are peer-oriented, so goals and tasks are organized by collaboration instead of receiving "sermon on the Mount" orders. The Scrum team has three key roles to it.

Each has an important role to play, and each of them must be present in a Scrum team.

1. Product Owner

As you've probably guessed, this is the owner of the final product on a Scrum team. How the role is conducted may differ from owner to owner and project to project, but those in this role have specific responsibilities.

The product owner is solely in control of the product backlog, updating it as needed to adjust to new situations and client requests. They are the ones who would prioritize the backlog in the best way that will achieve the goal. They ensure that it's transparent to all, including the client, and that it's clear what the development team will work on next.

The product owner is all about the "why" of the project. They're promoting the customer's needs and ensuring the customer's requirements are met with each feature.

Only one person can be the product owner, and they will be the ones held accountable for the product. If the development team doesn't get it right, it's still the product owner whom the client will hold responsible.

Given this accountability, the product owner must be a person respected by all on the team and the stakeholder. They must have the courage to step forward when needed and accept the blame for a failed product if it comes to that.

2. Scrum Master

The Scrum master is more like a coach facilitating the Scrum team. They're often the project manager, but don't necessarily have to be. Because the Scrum master doesn't have any expressed authority, they're more in a servant-leadership position.

They're crucial to improving the productivity of the Scrum development team. Officially, they also facilitate team meetings: daily Scrum, retrospectives, planning sessions, etc. Besides, they maintain the Scrum board. They're there to encourage the team to be better and improve their work.

They clear the way for the team to work efficiently and effectively. They may be required to sort out obstacles that arise, and they help promote communication among the team and with the client. It's also their role to protect the team from outside distractions. They don't commit the team to anything without consulting them first.

The Scrum master needs to be an expert in Scrum practices, as well as a good communicator and collaborator. Because they protect the team, they need to be able to stand up to outside pressure to allow the team to work unimpeded.

3. Development Team

The development team makes up every member of a Scrum project team. It's self-organized, meaning no one tells the team members how to do their work, not even the Scrum master! In Scrum, all are peers.

There are also no sub-teams because the development team is cross-functional. It must include everyone necessary to plan, design, produce, test, and release the product. They're doing the work that's required to finish the product increment and call it Done. They are the "how" of the project.

The team has to be large enough to complete the work during a sprint but stay small enough to handle change and be nimble. Fewer than three members often result in lowered productivity, but more than nine makes the team unwieldy ("What is a Scrum Development Team?" n.d.).[13] The product owner and Scrum master are separate from this count unless they're actively involved in performing specific sprint tasks.

Advantages of Scrum

As with all methodologies, there's no one perfect way to manage all projects. Many modern projects are well-suited to agile, even if they're not IT, and will also benefit from the Scrum structure.

- **Products are delivered quickly and effectively**

New releases or new features are ready at the end of each sprint. While the final product may not be available until the end of the project, versions of the product can be released to obtain market share or get feedback from users. The client knows what the end of each sprint will be and can arrange their marketing and sales operations accordingly.

- **The structure helps waterfall project managers ease into agile**

Traditional project managers are used to instructing from the top down and are not as comfortable with the fast-paced world of agile. Being able to plan the sprints in combination with the team will give them some relief that planning is being done. This is even if it's in a more collaborative setting, and they're aware that the situation may change rapidly.

Daily and review meetings are also forms of structure. These often have more stakeholder presence than a waterfall project manager is accustomed to, though it does give them a chance to be updated on each member's progress, which would otherwise be memorialized in a Gantt chart.

- **Good for fast-moving projects**

The short duration of the sprints means that the project can evolve as necessary with the changing conditions. The client may be in a hurry to get their product out to market before competitors can take away their market share. Being able to release at the end of the sprints and remove the long waterfall process is especially helpful in these types of situations.

- **No surprises for stakeholders**

  The client doesn't have to worry about ending up with a completely different product without seeing the process for months on end. Stakeholders are involved throughout, reviewing outputs from each sprint and can be present in sprint planning sessions and daily stand-ups. They know where the product is in the process and why it's there. There's less chance of being blindsided by a large resource task.

- **Clear visibility**

  In addition to the visibility that the stakeholders have, the entire team also understands the process. They have been instrumental in the resource estimation and the sprint planning, rather than leaving it up to the project manager, as is the case with a traditional project manager.

  While the product owner is responsible for the product, all the team members know the why and how for each individual sprint. They're not being given top-down instructions, but have self-organized to make the most of each team member's skills and capabilities that are necessary for the user story.

- **Individual productivity is apparent, and everyone is held accountable**

  Every day, each team member must stand up and describe the day's work and what they want to accomplish for the next. No one gets to rest on their laurels or skate by on another team member's abilities. It's immediately obvious if they were slacking off or if they got their work done as expected.

Disadvantages of Scrum

- **Lack of end date contributes to scope creep**

  Scrum makes it very easy to add features, user stories, and sprints continuously. Because there's no end date—as is typical in waterfall—there's no reason to stop if the team or product owner can find another user story or feature.

  To avoid scope creep, it's crucial for all involved to maintain discipline. Limit the scope to the user stories specified initially.

- **Requires commitment from all**

  A Scrum team is self-organizing, which means team members assign tasks and responsibilities themselves. As a result, no member should slack off or stop using Scrum, its values, and its pillars. Everyone must remain open to collaboration and communication while rolling with the punches. Everyone must contribute to the best of their ability.

  It also requires the stakeholders to be committed to Scrum. It may be difficult for customers who are used to the traditional waterfall approach, in which there is a project manager to rely on to organize a team as it goes along. While they may enjoy the visibility into the process that they never had with a traditional project, they may not be prepared for the amount of communication that's required with Scrum.

  They can't give up Scrum once there's an issue with one of the sprints or stop being available for team questions during sprint planning. They *must* commit to Scrum all the way through.

- **Must have a knowledgeable Scrum master for new teams**

  Scrum is simple but not always easy, especially for recent

waterfall converts. While an existing team that already works well together may not require a Scrum master, a new team definitely will.

The Scrum master needs to be exactly that: a *master*. They need to know how to foster collaboration among people who may not know each other well and handle the interaction between the team and the stakeholder. They must grasp their function as a coach and not a project manager nor a product owner. They have to be able to handle the process questions from the team and be willing to dive in whenever their team needs them. They also must be capable of blocking outside interference, no matter where it comes from, so their team can get on with the required work.

These skills only come with experience as a Scrum master. A bad Scrum master, or none at all when one is needed, can tank a project.

- **All must have good communication skills**

One benefit of a traditional project is that everyone knows what they're doing at any given time, and they know it upfront. The client is left outside the process until the very end when the product is delivered, except for with a few update meetings. Thus, the team members can pretty much be left alone to do their own thing as the project progresses.

This is not so with Scrum. The product manager has to know if one of the tasks is running behind or if the team member has a question about it. The client is continuously kept informed of progress, along with any questions on the way. The team members may be in communication with other project teams as well if an issue arises that's been dealt with before.

There's no member of a Scrum team that can be left in isolation when doing tasks. Team members may not communicate well with others because they lack the skills or willingness, and the team's chemistry may not work. Since communication skills are critical, the presence of any of these problems may inadvertently damage a relationship through thoughtless or ill-timed messages.

- **If one member leaves, the project is in danger**

Scrum teams should be relatively small, so they stay nimble. Most members have experience in several areas since the teams are cross-functional. In other words, if one person leaves, more than one piece of the puzzle may be going with them.

The sprints are planned tightly, so losing one person would create a huge hole in the productivity of the team. Either the rest of the team has to scramble to fill it, or they have to hunt down another team member to take care of it. The new member must then be brought up to speed, which may require more time for them to learn how to collaborate best with the existing team.

Key Takeaways

Scrum is the most popular agile framework, but a successful project requires a certain amount of maturity and communication from all team members.

- There are many reasons why Scrum is the most popular agile methodology, including its simplicity and the ease of transition from waterfall projects.
- Scrum is built on three pillars: transparency, inspection, and adaptation; and five additional values: commitment, openness, focus, respect, and courage.
- The Scrum team is made up of the product owner, Scrum master, and development team.
- Scrum terminology includes the following three artifacts: product backlog, sprint backlog, and product increment.
- Scrum practice includes developing a product backlog, sprint planning session that produces the sprint backlog, execution of the plan with daily Scrum meetings, and review session at the end of the sprint.
- The advantages of Scrum involve collaboration, transparency, and a fast time to market, whereas the disadvantages include the team structure and the high communication requirements.

In the next chapter, you will learn about other agile frameworks and where they can be used best.

---

[10] https://**www.techwell.com**/2013/02/why-Scrum-so-popular

[11] https://**www.mountaingoatsoftware.com**/agile/user-stories

[12] https://**www.altexsoft.com**/blog/business/25-Scrum-process-best-practices-that-set-your-agile-workflow-for-efficiency/

[13] https://**www.Scrum.org**/resources/what-is-a-Scrum-development-team

CHAPTER 7

BUT WAIT, THERE'S MORE!

IN addition to Scrum, there are a variety of other agile methodologies that project teams can use. Each has its own advantages and disadvantages, which make them more suited to certain types of projects and less for others. Some people may find that they prefer one over another because it suits the way they like to work better. In this chapter, we'll discuss five of the more popular ones that you may come across in your career in project management.

Methodology refers to the outline of the project's management principles, essential values, and best practices. It contains the goal of the project. By contrast, the *framework* is how to achieve the goal and the process for following the methodology.

Kanban

This is an agile framework for improving workflow and not a comprehensive project management methodology. It relies on visual tools to help teams find bottlenecks and manage them. A process must be in place before they can use Kanban. Some Scrum teams use Kanban as well. Teams use a **Kanban board**, which shows tasks that are Ready, In Progress, and Completed. The board is divided into "swim lanes," so tasks can move from one swim lane to the next, as appropriate. It's an evolutionary change that improves the existing workflow.

The key to Kanban is the concept of flow. Work should flow fairly smoothly through the swim lanes. If something is hindering the flow, the team will analyze it using various metrics and tools. As bottlenecks are discovered and removed, the process improves. It also emphasizes the need to keep changes moderate and manageable. Typically, Kanban is not used on its own but can be overlaid onto other methodologies–such as Scrum and waterfall–to make process improvements.

It's applied for achieving greater output while using fewer in-progress tasks, which makes it most suitable for projects that lean heavily on task prioritization, visualization, and streamlining. It's also suitable for projects where priorities may vary, and for production support.

In the last chapter, we discussed Scrum, and contrasting the two will help define both. While in Scrum, there are three defined roles (product owner, Scrum master, and development team), there are no specific roles in Kanban. These teams may have a project manager. However, all team members should jump in with any portion of the work when necessary.

There are no sprints in Kanban; everything is delivered when needed. This allows the team to pull more work when one piece is complete. The team makes gradual changes along the way where they see fit, so they can adapt quickly. This is in contrast with Scrum, where changes during the sprint aren't encouraged, and the adaptations wait until the next sprint. Productivity in Kanban is measured through cycle time, or the length of time required to finish the project from beginning to end.

Kanban's Six Core Practices

- **Visualize the workflow**

  Visualization is a fundamental step. Using a Kanban board, the team must lay out the process steps for the project they're working on (the Kanban board can be a whiteboard or digital in the PM software you're using.)

- **Limit work-in-progress (WIP)**

  Working only on one task at a time is known as a pull system: new work isn't pulled in by the team until the previous one is completed. You can achieve this by limiting the number of jobs in the WIP column on the Kanban board. When starting, it may not be clear exactly what the WIP limit should be. Teams often choose to limit it to 1 or 1.5 times the number of people in the team.

  Putting the limits on a Kanban board helps not just the team, but also the customers to know how much work the team can do in any given period. It helps set expectations. As Dr. Arne Roock says, the mantra needs to be "Stop starting! And start finishing!" ("What is Kanban?" n.d.).[14]

- **Control flow**

  After you've laid out your process steps and decided how to limit WIP, the team now can monitor the workflow. It may be moving smoothly within the set limits, or the work may start to pile up around a bottleneck.

The key to correcting the bottlenecks is to analyze how long the work items are in an intermediate wait or "handoff" stage. Being able to reduce the time spent in these stages will also help correct the bottlenecks.

- **Clarify policies and make them explicit**

  How the work gets done is clearly defined by each team in Kanban. This means everyone on the team knows how to perform the steps. The policies are guidelines for anything that can help the team manage the workflow on the board; for example, there is a clear definition for complete and swim lanes on the board (which may include To-Do, In Process, Completed, etc.). Everyone also knows who pulls work and when that is accomplished.

- **Create feedback loops**

  Feedback loops let the team know if they're making improvements as expected. Reports, metrics, and other visual tools can be used to make sure the team is on the right track. If they're headed in the wrong direction, feedback loops alert them sooner, so they can make changes more quickly.

- **Use experimentation and collaborative improvement**

  Gradual change is the way to evolve into a better process, always experimenting to see if it produces improvement. The scientific method is used to form a hypothesis and test it, in collaboration with the team. Small adjustments along the way lessen resistance to change, and visual signals from the Kanban tools provide feedback for whether your hypothesis is working or not.

Four principles of Kanban

1. Start where you are

Kanban encourages teams to start with what already exists, rather than making any adjustments right away. Over time, the team may introduce small changes intended to improve the workflow as they discover them.

2. Pursue incremental change

The idea is to make small changes that are absorbed easily and less subject to resistance from others within the organization. Big leaps are often viewed with suspicion, thus smaller adjustments are more likely to be welcomed.

3. Respect roles and titles initially

There's no need to make changes at the outset in terms of personal and roles, either. The team may decide to make changes later regarding roles and titles. They'll identify the needs as a team. This principle also helps to reduce the resistance to change often found in organizations.

4. All levels can be leaders

All team members should be encouraged to improve their leadership skills. Leadership isn't just a function of titles and is not restricted to those higher-ups in the organization.

Scrumban

You can probably guess what Scrumban is all about! Just as you suspected, it's the combination of the iterative Scrum processes with the visualization and gradual improvements of Kanban. There are similarities between the Scrum and Kanban flavors of agile, which allow them to work well together. In fact, the Scrum board was lifted from Kanban. Scrum sprints have defined endings, whereas Kanban limits their WIP. However, rather than having a definite end at one of the limits, the work flows into a new WIP.

The differences are exploited to make the project more productive and with less waste. As with Kanban, there are no defined team roles beyond a project manager. The Scrumban team does iteration planning (no longer sprint planning) at regular intervals to incorporate the review and retrospective meetings. Work is prioritized, so once the previous priority is completed, the team works with the next highest one. This may change along the way, and the Scrumban team adapts to that. There's an additional swim lane of "Ready" before the work is released.

The sprint backlog is limited in size instead of scope, which means WIP is also limited. Therefore, cycle time is more critical because each sprint should be pretty close in size to every other one. Quality control happens when the work moves into the last swim lane and, if it doesn't meet expectations, the team conducts a root-cause analysis to fix the issue. There's no estimation, as is used in Scrum. Instead, the team prioritizes the tasks to be pulled during the WIP.

Scrumban is excellent for service industries and maintenance-type projects, concepts with many or unexpected user stories, and new product development, including R&D, packaging, and delivery. It's also an excellent choice for a Scrum team or project that has workflow issues or problems with resources, among other challenges.

Lean

Lean similar to Kanban because it also focuses on the processes involved in the project. However, this one is aimed at continually improving the work that the entire organization performs. It seeks to eliminate waste by trimming the fat from bottlenecks and extra steps, transforming the project into Lean processes and products.

Waste can occur at any step of the way. It could be in the form of wait time, excess production, extra inventory, inferior quality products, too many steps in the process, or ineffective or costly transportation. It could also be the underuse of resources, such as human capital. Other waste products include excessive documentation, too many meetings, or unproductive multitasking.

This idea originated in Japan and became known as the Toyota Production System. Although it began in manufacturing, Lean has extended to many different industries, as the concept of focusing on human value and reducing waste is very attractive.

Five Principles for Lean

1. Specify values in the customer's eyes

Value is the capability provided to the customer for the right price at the right time. The critical point here is that the customer defines value, not the Lean team.

2. Identify the value stream

A value stream in manufacturing refers to all the actions that must be taken to deliver a product from raw materials to the customer. For IT and other industries, the value stream is the flow from the design concept to launch.

The stream can then be mapped out visually. First, "as-is": what the current process looks like. Then, the team would analyze it to find bottlenecks or other forms of waste. They use the analysis to create a future process map, where waste has been reduced or eliminated.

Finally, the team must create an improvement map: how they will get from current to future.

3. Eliminate the waste to create a workflow

Create a continuous workflow by eliminating stoppages, rework, interruptions, and the like. Each step falls into one category:

- **Value-adding**–these are the essential process steps that create and increase value, and the team should maximize their usage.
- **Value-enabling**–They do not create value for the customer. These may be required by current technology, legislation, company culture, or environment. Work in this category should be minimized as much as possible until it can be eliminated.
- **Non-value-adding**–These steps do nothing but add waste, so remove them as quickly as possible.

4. Customer priorities decide the pull

It's a saying in many service businesses that you want to underpromise and overdeliver. However, with Lean, you don't want to deliver value to the customer until they request it specifically–thus, deliver, not overdeliver. The initial scope should rule the process.

5. Set a goal for continuous improvement

Activities need to be evaluated constantly for their added value. It's the pursuit of perfection with the recognition that perfection may never be fully achieved.

The key to Lean is in the value stream mapping, which monitors how value is created. Materials and resources are allocated in the exact amounts and time when they're needed. Lean projects also require a degree of maturity, so the project stays agile–open to change,

communicating, and being visible to the client—while using Lean principles to eliminate waste.

Lean works well in manufacturing and other processes and industries that tend to build up a lot of waste products.

Six Sigma

If you've ever had a statistics class, you might guess what Six Sigma is all about. In an environment with a normal distribution (where the graph is shaped like a bell curve), there are two key statistics—the mean, which is basically the average of all the measurements, and the standard deviation, which is represented by the Greek letter *sigma*, σ, and is the variation from the mean. You can find 68% of all measurements within *one* standard deviation from the mean, in other words, plus or minus from that average. 99.73% of the measurements are within *six* standard deviations (three plus and three minus).

Motorola trademarked Six Sigma for their manufacturing process, where the measurements were defect-free components. In other words, 99.73% of their parts need to be free of defects and errors. Thus, the Six Sigma framework is intended to improve quality—and can be used in conjunction with Lean as well, forming ***Lean Six Sigma***—and deliver defect-free products or services to the customer.

There are two prongs to the solution when using this type of project management—first is to identify the problem, and the second is to solve the problem. There are two ways to deliver a Six Sigma project, depending on whether the project is an improvement for an existing product or service, or if it's a new design or significant re-design.

Six Sigma Process Steps

If the team is looking to improve customer satisfaction with an existing product, they can use the **DMAIC** model: **Define, Measure, Analyze, Improve, Control**.

However, if an existing process doesn't meet the customer's requirements, or if there is no product, the team should use **DMADV**: **Define, Measure, Analyze, Design, Validate**.

Six Sigma, like all agile methodologies and frameworks, is customer-centric as opposed to product-centric; therefore, the process begins from the customer's perspective. The first step is to **Define** the problem. The Voice of the Customer, a Six Sigma tool, is used here to help capture the client's needs.

Next, the team needs to **Measure** the problem. They will select metrics to confirm there's an improvement. Benchmarking is a standard Six Sigma tool to help teams measure their performance. They may benchmark against companies in a similar industry, between departments (internal benchmarking), or against competitors.

A common tool for measurement is the organization's "control chart," which is used to plot how the process changes over time. There's always an average line that may fluctuate, and upper and lower control limits, which come from historical data. This shows whether the current process is within limits or highly variable, which is an issue. Not all processes are measured in this way, but it is a useful tool.

The third step is to **Analyze** the current setup. Where do the inefficiencies lie? Historically, where have the variations come from? One of the most popular Six Sigma tools, Five Whys/Root Cause Analysis, is essential for this step. To determine the root cause of an issue, the team needs to ask why. When they come up with the first reason, they need to ask why again, and so forth. This process is called the

Five Whys, but it may take fewer or more to reach the root cause of the problem.

For example, suppose the project is to reduce worker's compensation claims at a healthcare facility. Analysis of the historical data shows that workers end up with shoulder soft tissue injuries in the records room. The team starts asking: Why does this happen? The workers have to pull large files. Why does this cause shoulder problems? Because the workers pull files out from drawers that are over their heads. Why do they do this? Because the file cabinets are too tall. Why don't they use the step stools? Because the step stools are located at the front of the room and too far away from the file cabinets for workers who are in a rush. Why are the stools at the front of the room? Because that's where maintenance puts them when they clean up at the end of the night.

Before the analysis, the team probably did not realize that the cause of shoulder injuries was where maintenance put step stools at the end of the night! As you can see, there are several solutions to this problem, though it's important to remember that everything has a cost. Technically, the workers are probably supposed to take their stools with them when they go to the stacks, and you may think that's the solution. In reality, it probably isn't, since they haven't been doing that historically. Another solution might be to lower the height of the filing cabinets, which would likely require a reconfiguration of the room and be expensive.

On the other hand, the company could—and probably should—digitize the records, so no one is pulling heavy files full of paper. There may be some obvious expenses with this solution, but if that's the direction the organization is headed in anyway, this would be a good solution. However, now you would need an interim solution, since it's not clear how long it will take before workers can stop pulling files, and you don't want more injuries in the meantime. You could instruct maintenance to place the stools closer to the file cabinets after they finish cleaning for the night, for example.

When the project team is working on an existing process, the next step is to **Improve** the current situation. Brainstorming is a standard tool for teams in this step for generating ways to make things better. They may also use the *5S System*, which is derived from Japanese manufacturing techniques to reduce bottlenecks and inefficiencies: Sort, Set in order, Shine, Standardize, and Sustain. Continuous improvement, known as Kaizen, is aimed at finding and reducing or eliminating waste and inefficiency constantly.

After the team makes the improvements, the process flows into the **Control** step, where the team ensures that the improvements are sustainable and whether the goal can be achieved. If so, the new process can be implemented.

If the team is working on something new, after they Analyze the situation, they must **Design** a new one (rather than Improving an existing one.) Once that step is complete, they need to **Validate** it. Similar to the Control step in the previous model, the team must be satisfied that the new process is sustainable and will achieve the objectives before they implement it.

A Six Sigma team requires some Six Sigma expertise to be successful. Just as the Scrum method has a Scrum master, Six Sigma has green, black, and master black belts. A team member new to Six Sigma is considered a white or yellow belt, but they'll need someone with more expertise on the team. Later in the book, we'll discuss the requirements for these standards. For now, know that a team can be led by a green belt or higher.

This methodology can be quite helpful when the project is about reducing errors or waste in a service or product. It can benefit companies in both strategic planning and employee motivation. Once

the SWOT (Strengths, Weaknesses, Opportunities, Threats) has been conducted as part of planning, the organization can use Six Sigma to work on the weaknesses. Using the methodology helps keep employees invested and interested in their work.

A variety of industries use Six Sigma—not just manufacturing companies. It helps increase customer satisfaction because it values customer input. Reducing waste and inefficiencies also shortens the cycle time for production, and some companies have seen reductions up to 35% (Dey, 2015).[15]

Extreme Programming (XP)

This framework is dedicated to software engineering. XP is the most specific framework when it comes to the process, so it's the most commonly used Extreme Programming "flavor." It is based on ***five values***.

1. Simplicity

Extreme programming requires that the simplest technique that will work be used. This strategy avoids waste and inefficiencies, especially overdesigning, which can be an issue in the software development community. Simpler technology can be installed and maintained easily. Address what's known only, without trying to predict the future.

2. Communication

Team members must communicate their knowledge with each other. Historically, this has meant face-to-face and working on white-boards rather than using project management software to create them digitally.

3. Feedback

The way to improve continuously is to gather and incorporate feedback during the process–not just at the end. It also contributes to simpler designs because the team can make adjustments based on feedback and not on guesses or estimates about the future.

4. Respect

Team members must respect each others' ideas and communications, along with the other values at the job.

5. Courage

This can also be viewed as "effective action in the face of fear." Each team member must have the courage to speak up about inefficiencies or waste they see in the work, so they can stop doing something that isn't working and change it, and also to accept and incorporate feedback.

Core Practices of XP

In addition to these five values, there is a set of core practices that Extreme Programming uses to make simple and useful software. Practice excellence is the key to this framework. The goal is to master them.

- **Sit Together**

  This one is pretty self-explanatory. The team should sit together with no barriers, not even cubicle walls.

- **Whole Team**

  Those with the need and those who will satisfy the need should always be working together.

- **Energized Work**

  Staying focused and distraction-free is inevitable for effective development. Each team member avoids overwork and remains healthy while encouraging the rest of the team the same.

- **Informative Workspace**

  The work of the team is transparent to all involved. There is some space available for when privacy is required.

- **Pair Programming**

  Two brains with four eyes are better than one brain with two eyes. In XP, two people would work together on production software and one machine. It provides continuous code review and, if one person gets stuck on a problem, there would be someone else there to help solve it. They stay more focused, so it takes less time to develop simple coding.

- **Weekly Cycle**

  This is the same as an iteration or sprint. The team would meet at the beginning of the week to review progress, and the customer would choose the next story to work on. The goal is to have code that realizes the story by the end of the week.

- **Quarterly Cycle**

  This is the equivalent of a release. At the beginning of the quarter, the customer explains which features they want to receive that quarter. The order of stories and when they get delivered may change within the quarter as it evolves.

- **Stories**

  User stories that describe what the software should do for customers.

- **Ten-Minute Build**

  This means to build the feature and test it in ten minutes or less. Builds that require more time are less likely to be tested regularly. That introduces a longer time to find and fix errors.

- **Slack**

  Similar to planning for a six-hour day. These are tasks that can easily be put aside if something more urgent comes up. Building slack tasks into the day ensures that there will be time to address surprises.

- **Continuous Integration**

  Immediately test the code when adding it, so if it doesn't work, it's much easier to fix. Most coders hate finding out that it doesn't work, so they try to avoid it by putting off testing. However, in XP, "If it hurts, do it more often" ("Extreme Programming, n.d.).[16]

- **Test-First Programming**

  Write a test first, run it, then develop code to make the test pass and re-run the test. Normally, developers would write code, write the tests, then run the test. When you test first, it accelerates the feedback cycle and reduces bugs.

- **Incremental Design**

  Do a little bit of work first to understand the overall design, but don't dive into a particular aspect until you're working on that feature. This helps avoid unnecessary changes made to the code, which tend to introduce more bugs.

Roles within XP

There aren't specific roles to an Extreme Programming team, but there are some common ones.

- **Customer**

  Because the process is customer-centric, their input is required for both weekly and quarterly cycles. They make the business decisions about the product and communicate this to other members of the team. Usually, several representatives from the customer are present to describe business requirements from all departments.

- **Developers**

  Most of the team (except for the customer, tracker, and coach) will be in this role. They're the ones realizing the stories. These roles are cross-functional, so there's no need for further role definition among the developers.

- **Tracker**

  One of the developers may be tasked as a tracker as well, who would keep tabs on the metrics and measure whether progress is being made as desired. Not all teams require a tracker.

- **Coach**

  A coach is, again, not a requirement, though teams new to the framework and XP, in particular, may want to add a coach to the team. Similar to a Scrum master, the coach has used Extreme Programming before and can coach the developers through it.

It's best used when the requirements for a software product are in a state of flux, projects with a fixed time requirement are too risky, the development team is relatively small and located near each other, and the technology allows for automated tests.

Choosing a Framework

So, which one should you use? The frameworks differ in their adaptability. That means that, while one framework might be perfect for one project, it might not be for the next. Also, there is no one-size-fits-all. The first thing you want to consider when choosing a framework is the needs of your project and your team.

As you've seen, they all have varying strengths and weaknesses. Agile frameworks have benefits for all kinds of industries, from manufacturing to service businesses, as well as different functions within organizations, from product development to IT to marketing and sales. Scrum, Lean, and Six Sigma focus on project management, while Extreme Programming is dedicated to software development specifically. You can also combine frameworks (Scrum + Kanban, Scrum + Lean, Six Sigma + Lean) depending on the needs of your project. This book focuses on agile frameworks, but some projects lend themselves to the traditional waterfall methodology instead.

Based on the Project Management Institute's Organizational Project Management Maturity Model (OPM3) and their practice guide, there are seven guidelines for choosing a framework ("Project Management Frameworks," n.d.).[17]

1. Examine the project size and scope.

If it's unclear exactly how big the project is and what the priorities are, it's likely a better candidate for an agile project rather than a traditional one. However, if it's going to be a large project that takes

a long time, you might be unable to break it down easily into biweekly or even monthly sprints.

2. What's the business case and value to the organization?

If you're planning to undertake a large project, make sure you know what the value drivers are. What are the benefits of doing this project, and will they outweigh the costs in terms of time and money?

3. As they say in banking and finance, Know Your Customer.

What are the pain points driving the project? What are their priorities, and what do they expect to gain from the project?

4. Once you understand the client's expectations, determine if any of their goals or outcomes is dependent on a specific framework.

Shifting priorities indicate agile and most likely something along the lines of Kanban. Are they frustrated with waste products or inefficiencies in their process? Now you're looking into Lean and Six Sigma as possibilities, and maybe a combo of the two. For software development, Extreme Programming may be the tack to take.

5. Now that you've analyzed which drivers may be better suited to each framework, list the potential methodologies and compare them with the drivers.

This could be a simple chart with the drivers and outcomes listed down the page, and your methodologies or frameworks across the top. Look at each row to see if the selected framework supports that particular item directly. You might find it helpful to check off each one that matches, so you can quickly see which project management method checks off more value drivers.

6. At this point, you should be able to see which methodology matches the client's needs and expectations best.

You probably won't have all the boxes checked. Take another look at your list and verify which value drivers are critical. For example, the client may want to reduce production cycle time, eliminate inefficiencies in the process, and reduce manufacturing costs by 25%. The cost reduction is most critical, so the framework you choose must address that goal directly. That could mean that you don't choose the one with the most checkmarks because, if it omits the most critical value driver of the project, you can't use it. Ideally, your framework will produce the best results with the lowest amount of risk; however, that's measured specifically for each particular project.

7. Choosing a framework is not the end of the road.

That's because you have to monitor the efficiency as you implement it. Since agile is all about flexibility and adaptability, you can throw in modifications to the framework or change it entirely if it doesn't produce the results you're looking for.

Key Takeaways

Different "flavors" of agile methodology work best on some projects, though not necessarily on others. Choosing the right framework is largely a matter of understanding the customer's needs and what will produce the best results with the lowest risk. Since agile frameworks are based on similar concepts, they can also be combined for a hybrid methodology.

- Kanban is a framework used frequently in conjunction with other agile frameworks and focuses on incremental change with visualization.
- Scrumban combines Scrum and Kanban and is useful for teams that face resource challenges, along with maintenance projects and new product development.
- Lean is based on Japanese just-in-time practices and helps eliminate waste in the process, especially (but not exclusively) for manufacturing. It is often combined with Six Sigma.
- Six Sigma is another project framework that eliminates waste and inefficiencies, and is helpful when the client has an existing process that needs to be modified or re-designed.
- Extreme Programming is a way to eliminate waste and inefficiencies in software development.

In the next chapter, you will learn about agile project methodology.

---

[14] https://**www.digite.com**/kanban/what-is-kanban/
[15] https://**www.greycampus.com**/blog/quality-management/why-should-you-choose-six-sigma
[16] https://**www.agilealliance.org**/glossary/xp/
[17] https://**www.wrike.com**/project-management-guide/project-management-frameworks/

CHAPTER 8

METHOD TO THE AGILE MADNESS

THERE are many "flavors" in Agile, but they're all based on the same principles of Agile. Because these techniques have been in use for some time, there's a manifesto of the principles underlying all Agile projects. Now there are best practices as well, and experience with overcoming common hurdles.

Agile Manifesto

In 2001, a group of agile project managers from a variety of disciplines–Extreme Programming, Scrum, etc.–gathered together and hammered out a manifesto of what should guide all agile project teams.[18] These principles are the foundation of any Agile project, no matter which framework the team has chosen. It's helpful to read the manifesto several times for a stronger understanding of the core principles of agile project management.

1. Our highest priority is to satisfy the customer through early and continuous delivery of a valuable product.
2. Welcome changing requirements, even late in development. Agile processes harness change for the customer's competitive advantage.
3. Deliver projects frequently, from a couple of weeks to a couple of months, with a preference to the shorter timescale.
4. Business people and team members must work together daily throughout the project.
5. Build projects around motivated individuals. Give them the environment and support they need, and trust them to get the job done.
6. The most efficient and effective method of conveying information to and within a development team is face-to-face conversation.
7. A working product is the primary measure of progress.
8. Agile processes promote sustainable development. All stakeholders and team members should be able to maintain a constant pace indefinitely.
9. Continuous attention to technical excellence and good design enhances agility.
10. Simplicity—the art of maximizing the amount of work not done—is essential.
11. The best architectures, requirements, and designs emerge from self-organizing teams.
12. At regular intervals, the team reflects on how to become more effective, then tunes and adjusts its behavior accordingly.

APM Best Practices

Now that agile is spread across the world, we have been able to codify some of the best practices. Remember that a critical value in APM is communication, so it shouldn't be too surprising that agile project managers and teams share their experiences amongst each other to help everyone achieve their goals.

The following practices are summarized in the *7 Best Practices of the Agile Project Manager Checklist*. I believe these are the most critical aspects every successful project manager should follow because it is easy to forget some until they become habits. You can highlight those where you need to improve and focus on them daily. You will be surprised how following these simple but powerful practices may improve your project success rate. You will find a link at the beginning of this book that will lead you to download the checklist.

- **Develop iterative processes**

  Break down the work into manageable chunks. They don't need to be ordered linearly unless the tasks are dependent on each other, but they should occur in terms of priority.

- **Collaborate with the customer**

  Working together with the customer and asking for regular feedback will improve the chances of success for any project significantly. When the customer has visibility into the work, it helps them manage their expectations, and they can know the project team is doing their best work. It also ensures the team knows what's important to the customer, so they can deliver valuable, high priority, and high-quality products.

- **Tweak the product backlog with the customer**

  In the way of collaborating with the customer, special attention should be paid to the product backlog. The team gets a good handle on what is essential to the customer and can fine-tune it to ensure they're meeting the right goals.

- **Meet daily**

  This will help the team and the customer understand where they are on the project, including who's on track or not, and who needs help. It also clarifies for the team members what they should be working on next.

  Customers should be invited to these meetings as well. It manages their expectations and helps them understand how the team works, thus helping them give better feedback as well.

- **Use the right tools for the job**

  PM software is inevitable for many project teams, particularly those who aren't geographically close to one another and still need to communicate in real time. It automates manual and tedious tasks, freeing up team members' time to do meaningful work.

  Charts and visual aids are important for everyone to see what's going on with the project. Teams can track sprint velocity, burndown rates, schedules, and cycle times very easily. Tracking essential metrics helps the team ensure they are doing the right task at the right time, and can, therefore, adjust if they're not or when plans need to change.

- **Use the right people for the job in self-organizing teams**

  Agile requires team members to be mature, know how to com-

municate, have whatever specialized skills or knowledge as needed, and be motivated to achieve the customer's goals through their work. Teams don't need to wait for someone "on high" to tell them what to do next–they can figure it out themselves and distribute the work equally according to each members' individual knowledge and experience.

Invest in your team and plan team-building activities and spaces for them to get to know each other better. These activities are not only enjoyable, but they can help lift the performance of your team to the next level.

- **Reflect to improve**

  An agile team always wants to get better, which includes reducing errors, cycle time, waste, and inefficiency, and achieve the client's goals in a faster and smarter way. Spending time at the end of each sprint or iteration and reflecting on what could have been better helps teams collect what they've learned in time to deploy them for the next sprint.

  A well-known management consulting firm uses "Plus/EBIs" for this process. They discuss what went well–Plus, then they talk about what would have been "Even Better Ifs,"–EBIs.

  Whatever method you choose, implement it regularly and consistently to reap the benefits of continuous improvement. Perform the lessons learned after the whole project has finished.

Overcoming Hurdles

While APM is better for projects that require adaptability and flexibility, there are still some common hurdles that Agile teams would face.

- **Company structure doesn't support Agile**

  Some managers, usually those who are fond of command-and-control structures, find waterfall much easier to understand, mainly because of waterfall's more linear process. They may not understand the benefits of agile or how self-organizing teams can work.

  Building a business case and developing support from key influencers in the company will help here. There needs to be buy-in for agile at a higher level to maintain the close client-team relationship that agile requires.

- **Rushed testing**

  Fast sprints often lead to a rushed testing cycle, which then results in overseen bugs and defects. Building the testing into the sprint and in software and writing the tests first (as in Extreme Programming) will help ensure a robust test to find and squash as many bugs as possible.

- **Unclear benefits to the business**

  Using APM won't guarantee that the project will help the company achieve strategic goals. The agile project must be used as part of a strategic business case to do its job properly and show the company that agile is a reliable methodology to use. Remember that project management is the primary tool for a company to achieve its strategic goals.

- **Limited agile skills available**

  This is probably less true in IT, but, in other industries, project managers and teams are usually more used to waterfall projects. In other words, there are fewer agile project managers and team

members with the skills necessary to implement a successful agile project than the demand.

In this case, the company may wish to either retrain existing traditional teams or select candidates for agile training. We will discuss more about the specific certifications in chapter ten. If you and your company can't hire the capability, you will have an opportunity to build it.

- **The agile planning need is underestimated**

Because the entire project isn't planned out at the beginning as would be in waterfall PM, some may have an illusion that there isn't any proper planning in APM. As the old adage goes, *failing to plan is planning to fail.*

At the beginning of the project, the team and the client should agree on the scope. They should flesh out a framework of what needs to be done and when. Once the project begins, each sprint or iteration is planned before the team executes it.

- **Teams aren't well-planned or executed**

Because the agile team is self-organizing and often cross-functional, the key to success lies in a strong, motivated team with complementary skill sets.

Teams that have worked together successfully in the past are best, but if one is not available, care should be taken in selecting each individual member. All need to have the maturity to step in and do whatever work is required to communicate with others.

- **Limited understanding of the project focus or scope**

Not understanding the scope of the project or how it fits into the customer's business leads to being unable to tell when the project's finished, along with a potential failure to meet the client's goals and expectations.

The APM team must understand how the work feeds into the customer's mission, values, and business goals. This provides the scope and leads to a higher likelihood of success.

- **Limited customer feedback**

  The customer is key to an agile project, so limiting their feedback or even disregarding it will likely result in project failure, in which the end result does not meet the client's goals.

  An APM team will want its products to be useful and wasteless, and to have that, the customer must provide feedback to help them head down the right track. The most spectacular feature a coder can design means nothing if it doesn't achieve the customer's strategic objectives.

When APM Is the Right Fit

By now, you probably recognize that APM is a great tool to use when the project needs to adapt to changes in customers' requirements, situations, and dynamic industry environment. Using agile helps the company bring the product to market faster, which then increases their return on investment. Using the iterative process helps IT organizations, in particular, release software with fewer bugs.

We've also discussed the need for team members to be mature problem solvers by nature. What might not have been clear is that many team members are *happier* under an agile environment, given their necessary maturity and skillset. Agile projects provide the team with an opportunity to manage their own tasks and exert a sense of control over their workflow, which is an aspect of agile that, studies have shown, makes people happier (Rayome, 2018).[19]

With all these benefits, there are still companies and situations in which traditional PM would make more sense. Some organizations, such as government entities, operate within narrow or rigid legal or regulatory boundaries. They're often better off with waterfall and its extensive documentation practices. If there are good reasons for not using more flexible frameworks, the organization will likely still need to stick to the traditional methodology.

Most companies, however, will benefit from how agile helps them adapt to new environments. The biggest obstacles to adopting agile are organizational culture and behavior (Rayome, 2018).[20] The whole company must buy into using flexible practices and self-organizing teams. Those with legacy command-and-control structures have difficulty trusting their people to figure out a reasonable schedule or budget, then stick to it.

To work well, all levels of an organization must support and promote the agile way of working on projects, including senior management.

At the department level, agile works best with managers and employees who are unafraid of change. Humans have a natural resistance to change; however, as long as the department is willing to try new things, then agile will be more likely to be successful. A whole department of those who fear change will be extremely difficult to convert. In this situation, Kanban and its approach to gradual and incremental change may eventually win them over.

In addition, if the work in the department is less rigid, agile will not come as such a shock to the workers. However, in a place where work is highly structured and the employees are not incentivized or rewarded for independent thinking, it will be quite difficult to introduce APM for new projects.

Software development is the most obvious arena to begin with APM because requirements are always changing, and the nature of the business is already fast-paced. In the past, many thought agile was best for co-located teams that could do the daily stand-ups in the same room. However, with the advent of remote work and social distancing, it's not clear whether that will continue to be the case. More teams may use web conference software to conduct stand-ups, even if most of the team is off-site.

Agile success also hinges on the willingness of stakeholders to be involved directly and consistently on the project. The team works best with real-time feedback, which allows them to hone the features down to match the customer's needs. In traditional PM, however, stakeholders may be invited to some status meetings, but they have no visibility into the project. If the organization has stakeholders who prefer to be hands-off, the development team will have a difficult time getting the necessary feedback and will likely end up wasting too much time.

Failure is crucial to agile success, which may seem counterintuitive to those who aren't familiar with it! However, failing fast and learning from those failures is how an agile team can move quickly and be adaptable. Large Silicon Valley firms adapted the fail-fast motto years ago, though the rest of corporate America hasn't necessarily caught up. This may cause a problem for company managers who frown on failure from their direct reports but are expected to welcome it from the project management team.

Key Takeaways

Though APM is a flexible methodology that works in many different functions and a variety of industries, there are times and places where traditional PM will fit better, or the adoption of agile will be an uphill battle because the organizational culture does not support it.

- The Agile Manifesto provides 12 principles that guide all APM projects, no matter the industry, functional area, or framework in use.
- Best practices for agile support the flexibility and responsiveness to change that are key to successful projects.
- Common hurdles often result from the difference between traditional and agile projects, and may require additional training or cultural buy-in to solve.
- Agile will be great for a good number of projects, as long as the team members can think independently, and the culture supports the communication and fail-fast objectives of APM.

In the next chapter, you will learn more about real-life Agile projects.

---

[18] https://agilemanifesto.org/principles.html

[19] https://www.techrepublic.com/article/how-to-tell-if-agile-is-the-right-project-management-style-for-your-business/

[20] https://www.techrepublic.com/article/how-to-tell-if-agile-is-the-right-project-management-style-for-your-business/

CHAPTER 9

THE GOOD, THE BAD, AND THE UGLY: AGILE PROJECT EXAMPLES

AT this point, you should have a good understanding of the benefits of agile and what it takes to do a successful agile project. Now, we'll discuss a variety of agile projects and what worked. Even more importantly, we will see what didn't work and caused the project to fail.

Everyday Uses of Agile

As noted earlier in the book, people often manage their own projects outside work or with specific work projects!

One example of a typical project that you could think of with an agile framework is remodeling your house. Rather than adjust everything at once, you can have the workers go room by room. Say you want to have the upstairs bathroom, downstairs bathroom, kitchen, and living room all redone. You would discuss the loose framework for what order the rooms should be tackled, an estimate of the budget, how long it may take, and how the redesigned rooms would fit into the house. This is the project planning.

The first sprint, or iteration, would be the upstairs bathroom. You and the contractor would discuss how you want the room to look and whether you need to remove walls to enlarge it or change its shape. This is your sprint planning. The contractor is an expert on how the room will be redone, but you're giving them the features you want to see in the end product.

It's your house, and you have a full stake in the final version. Therefore, you would monitor it pretty closely and, if the workers install the tiles incorrectly or put the tub in the wrong place, you would give them that feedback immediately! Afterward, they make the necessary corrections and move on. Once it's completed to your satisfaction, the team heads to the next room, and so forth.

Now that many of us are working from home, agile can increase our personal productivity as well. What you want to get accomplished or the goal you're seeking to achieve is your product backlog. Break down the steps into weekly sprints. At the beginning of the week—or the end of the previous one, which is my personal preference—you would plan the next week's tasks and what you want to have achieved by the end of it.

Limit your WIP, so you're not overwhelmed by too many tasks. Note that multi-tasking is not cognitively possible. What happens instead is that your brain switches between tasks constantly, which tires it out and leads to poorer decisions. Instead, manage your product and sprint backlogs, so you're not trying to work on too much at once. Try to give yourself blocks of time for uninterrupted, deep work. That was how I wrote this book, in fact—in blocks of time in which I did nothing else but write.

You may not need to have daily stand-ups with yourself (if you do, go for it), but you should make sure you're planning out enough time for the reflection and retrospective at the end of your week. What went well? What could have gone better? Various online tools can help with this, but many paper planners and journals will also contain space for this reflection as well.

Weddings may not be an everyday occurrence for most people (other than wedding planners!), but planning one is also an excellent time to use APM. Most couples find that all sorts of things come up, so there's a frequent need for course correction. Some tasks are dependent on others; for example, the wedding venue must be selected before the caterers and decorators. On the other hand, other tasks may occur concurrently, since flowers can be ordered while the catering is arranged. A burndown chart is excellent for measuring if everything is being booked and coordinated on time.

Successful APM Projects

1. FBI's Sentinel Project

This project was intended to bring together all data on known terrorists in one place. The first project manager (traditional PM) achieved essentially no results for $400 million and was fired, stopping the project. Then, the FBI brought in an Agile Chief Information Officer and Chief Technology Officer to restart the project. With APM, it only took fifteen team members and $30 million to complete the project successfully (Sutherland, 2014).[21]

2. Vistaprint

This company had been using traditional PM for a while and, after analysis, found its product teams took an average 60 days from ideation to actual product delivery. Only about 40 hours of this time was real work because the lead time was 40 days. In today's world, that is way too slow. They adopted agile methodology, including Kanban, and reduced their lead time from 40 days down to 15 (Velasquez, 2018).[22]

3. Lonely Planet

Here's a department you may not have thought would benefit from agile: legal! The lawyers at Lonely Planet are one such group that incorporated APM into their workload. They also provide guidance for business strategy in addition to developing contracts. They use a Kanban board and some Scrum methods to keep track of deliverables as they're worked on and completed. These lawyers prioritize their work and adapt as the priorities change. They've improved their productivity by 25% using APM (Bidwe, 2019).[23]

4. Spotify

The major companies that Spotify competes against, such as Google, have incorporated agile into their product development, running millions of automated tests a day on their code. Spotify hires Scrum masters that are also agile coaches to move faster and be nimbler than their competitors. They have multiple Scrum teams that deploy their pieces of software in sprints without interfering with the other teams. This allows them to stay ahead of the competition by deploying multiple times a day (Sutherland, 2014).[24]

5. National Public Radio

National Public Radio has been able to reduce its programming budget by one-third using agile techniques (Bidwe, 2019).[25] They began running small pilots with reduced staff first instead of rolling out full programs to test whether the programs would be successful. They gather feedback from the local outlets and listeners before increasing the size of the program.

Agile Projects That Failed

1. Healthcare.gov

Obamacare was initially a bit of a mess, having been based on waterfall that (unsurprisingly) failed. However, they left the front end, or the user experience, as agile. The back end was where the problem was because the deadlines had been missed so terribly that there were only six days to test it before it went live.

Having the back end in a different methodology was a failure to comply with the third principle in the Agile Manifesto, which specifies working software. Even though the front end was usable, the entire project was not working software.

2. Original ING Agile Rollout

Although ING has since made adjustments to how they work with agile, in the early years and after widespread adoption, senior management discovered they weren't reaping the benefits they had expected (Siroky, 2020).[26] Although individual projects succeeded, they did not see the gains in business outcomes. The business was still using traditional software delivery methods, which wiped out the gains seen from agile software development.

In other words, the whole culture wasn't practicing agile, and they didn't have buy-in at all levels.

3. Scrum Project in the Energy Sector

The scheduling software project was initially estimated to take a year to complete. Instead, it ended up taking three years and five times the initial budget.

Two vendors provided Scrum teams that failed to communicate with each other as needed, ending in an *us vs. them* mentality. The daily meetings turned into problem solving instead of the 15-minute stand-ups. Lessons learned from retrospectives weren't implemented and, as the project fell behind schedule, these meetings disappeared altogether. The Scrum master wasn't co-located and didn't keep track of what was happening. The product owner had to divide their time between the two vendors, so one was on hold while they were at the other, and vice versa. Company management canceled sprint reviews when one of them didn't meet their expectations.

Requirements were also a big issue for the project. The client had collected enormous documentation; however, when it came time for the project to launch, it was clear they were outdated. The client didn't want to collect any new documentation because they already had so much. Since so much was provided upfront, the client did not want to agree to any changes (Rajpal, 2016).[27]

This failure shows the importance of having all levels of client management on board with agile, maturity of the team members, and why communication is so important.

4. UK Government's Welfare Reform

The audit found that the IT project was too ambitious in its scope, and they were inexperienced with the agile methodology they chose. They didn't have an adequate plan or controls and were unable to measure their progress; thus, the project was not completed despite how it ran over budget (Universal Credit; Rajpal, 2016).[28]

Not having agile experts can be a huge problem, especially when the team members working on the project are unfamiliar with it and don't understand how it works.

5. UK Regional Department IT Project for Distributing Grants

The client was bureaucratic and had rigid structures for work in place, which, in general, would often lead to a culture of blame. Software developers chose agile to deliver the project. You may already see the issue that cropped up between blame-driven decision making and the fast iterations that are normal in APM. The key stakeholders were used to being in control and weren't able to let that go.

With agile projects, there needs to be trust between the team and the stakeholders. The stakeholders themselves didn't trust each other—also common in command-and-control hierarchical structures—much less the team. The developers didn't understand the requirements thoroughly, so they could not bring about the result the stakeholders expected. Instead, they focused on a different area of the project, which further eroded trust.

The team couldn't get the client to prioritize because the individual stakeholders would not agree to sprints in which their specific agenda took a back seat. They didn't want to make decisions because they could be blamed if things went wrong, which hindered the project development. Payments were delayed because the software wasn't delivered on time.

Given all this, however, the development team and the client both agreed that the project would have been canceled outright had they used a traditional waterfall model (Berger, 2007).[29]

6. Video Game Development

In one case, a team kept making more features with every sprint, and the product owner did not provide any feedback. The owner didn't attend the daily stand-ups or the reviews and limited user stories that the team needed for development. In addition, the product owner's vision wasn't communicated to internal customers, such as the marketing department, either. On viewing the final result, top management was shocked by how far off the game was from what they had envisioned ("User Stories," n.d.).[30]

What we have here is a failure to communicate.

7. Web-Based Reservation System

This agile team got off to a good start by doing their research into agile and certifying some of the team members as Scrum masters. They built the first version quickly and it worked well. Because it was so positive, the Scrum master didn't hold sprint retrospective meetings. Everything was going well, so why did the team need to talk about it?

Over time, however, the system slowed down to the point where it seemed to be moving backward. The codebase was increasing, which caused the system to become shaky. Company management eventually canceled the project.

This project started strong but fizzled out because a vital part of the sprint was ignored. Continuing the retrospectives might have enabled the team to spot the issues before the code lost its stability ("User Stories," n.d.).[31]

Key Takeaways

Most of the failures are the other side of the coin from the successes: when teams are unable to work collaboratively or to communicate, the projects fail. Interestingly, it's not APM specifics that lead to failure, but misapplication or organizational culture issues that prevent teams from successfully working with the stakeholders of a project.

- You can use agile principles and methodologies in everyday life.
- Agile projects have been successful in different types of industries and a variety of functional areas within companies.
- Agile project failures are mainly due to issues of culture and communication rather than with the steps or principles themselves.

In the next chapter, you will discover how to become the ideal project manager.

---

[21] https://openviewpartners.com/blog/agile-done-right-agile-gone-wrong/#.XqClIJIIA2w
[22] https://www.growthaccelerationpartners.com/blog/agile-development-real-world/
[23] https://www.synerzip.com/blog/4-examples-of-agile-in-non-technology-businesses/
[24] https://openviewpartners.com/blog/agile-done-right-agile-gone-wrong/#.XqClIJIIA2w
[25] https://www.synerzip.com/blog/4-examples-of-agile-in-non-technology-businesses/
[26] https://www.plutora.com/blog/agile-devops-failing-fortune-500-companies-wake-call-us
[27] https://link.springer.com/chapter/10.1007/978-3-319-33515-5_21
[28] https://www.nao.org.uk/report/universal-credit-early-progress-2/
[29] https://dx.doi.org/10.1016/j.ijinfomgt.2007.08.009
[30] https://www.mountaingoatsoftware.com/agile/user-stories
[31] https://www.mountaingoatsoftware.com/agile/user-stories

CHAPTER 10

THE IDEAL AGILE PROJECT MANAGER

ARE you ready to become an agile project manager? Whether you have a background in waterfall or you're new to project management, you should now have a better idea of the different frameworks and how they differ from traditional PM. What makes an excellent project manager?

Leadership Skills, Not Technical Skills

As you've seen, there are several ways that agile teams organize themselves. Yet, none of them require specific coding backgrounds for software development, expertise in making charts, or years of being a project manager. You don't need to be the best at Kanban boards, even if you're leading a project that uses Kanban, nor is there a particular class that you must take to master daily stand-ups or become a killer sprint reviewer.

Agile projects require proficiency in communication and personal maturity, above all, for all the team roles. Both of these are general leadership skills that you won't need to take a course or certification to master. You also won't need to possess a specific title or be at a certain level of the company to gain these skills.

Instead, APM is based on principles and core values. These values include respecting yourself, team members, stakeholders, the agile framework you've chosen to use, along with the importance of planning and communication. This is something that anyone can do.

In other words, as long as you base all your project leadership on values and principles, the rest will follow. Hire good, knowledgeable, and mature people who have the background and experience for success, and you've increased your chances for a successful project without getting bogged down in credentials and titles.

Certifications

Having said that, some companies do look for project managers with credentials. New project managers sometimes feel more comfortable obtaining a certification before they jump straight into the agile waters.

The nonprofit Project Management Institute (PMI) was founded in 1969 and offers certifications in project management, one of which is a key qualification for US project managers: the Project Management Professional (PMP). It validates your experience and knowledge as a project manager.

PMI also provides the Certified Associate in Project Management (CAPM), which is not quite at the level of a project manager. Besides, you can obtain more specialized certifications, such as Professional

in Business Analysis (PMI-PBA), Risk Management Professional (PMI-RMP), etc. The organization also offers Agile Certified Professional (PMI-ACP) for those who specialize in the agile project methodology. You're required to take an exam and have worked a certain number of months of agile projects, depending on whether you have a college degree or not.

You can also find certifications for specific methodologies. Six Sigma training requirements are listed as "belts," in which a white or yellow belt is new to entry and may work on a Six Sigma team but not lead it. Green belts have hands-on project management experience with three years' full-time. They can provide guidance to black belt teams or projects with data and analysis; however, they can only lead green belt projects/teams.

Black belts have completed two Six Sigma projects, have a minimum of three years' full-time employment, lead teams, and coach and train project teams. Master black belts must have already achieved black belt status and shown either five years of full-time employment or the completion of ten Six Sigma projects. They have coached and trained green and black belts, have a portfolio of work, and have also worked as a Six Sigma strategist.

Note that the requirements for a Six Sigma black belt—who is often the project manager of a team—focus on requirements and experience. They don't key in on academic degrees; instead, they look to the Six Sigma teams that a potential black belt has worked on. The full-time requirement ensures that the applicant has been steeped in the Six Sigma methodology, which means they've attended plenty of stand-ups, reviews, and retrospectives and become comfortable communicating with any level of any organization.

Scrum projects don't always have project managers, but they do have Scrum masters, who can also be thought of as player-coaches. Many institutions provide Scrum master certifications, but a key credential is the Certified Scrum Master from Scrum Alliance. Achieving this requires training from an Agile coach or Scrum trainer and an exam, and there are continuing education credits you'll need to earn to keep that certification.

The mentioned certifications are recognized worldwide and are preferred by many local companies. Many employers and clients require the eligible candidates to have a certification, especially for senior positions.

Responsibilities as a Project Manager

No matter which framework you choose, the duties of a project manager are pretty similar across all the Agile models.

- **Managing people in highly changeable environments**

  The agile team is self-organizing, but a leader can help the team figure out what the next step is when there are any difficulties. The project manager helps the team figure out how to deliver the release of a feature on time.

- **Motivating the team**

  APM requires team members to figure out how to get the work done themselves. Sometimes it's hard or the team runs up against an obstacle, and it's not immediately obvious how they can adapt to and overcome. The project manager would help keep motivation high, so the team is continuously trying to improve and deliver to the customer's satisfaction.

- **Coaching**

  Leaders of any kind often need to coach their players. It may be working through one of the agile core principles, general work attitude, or approach to a specific task.

- **Managing issues and escalating appropriately**

  There are times when senior management must be involved. The project manager can often solve intra-team issues themselves, perhaps with some coaching of the members. However, when issues come up that the project manager and stakeholders cannot resolve, the project manager must know who to approach in the organization to take care of it.

- **Modifying workload to maintain the pace**

  Sometimes, although the distribution of work may seem equal, it isn't always in practice. The project manager can step in to redistribute it to ensure the project deadlines are met.

- **Building trust**

  The duty of creating and maintaining a trust bond between the agile team and client rests on the project manager. Trust is fragile and can be broken easily, so the leader needs to build it, then help maintain it. Customers lose trust when deadlines or other requirements are missed, so part of this job is to deliver what has been promised.

- **Communicating adjustments to stakeholders**

  Agile projects move fast, and what was known at the beginning of the iteration may undergo a change and require adjustments in the next. The project manager must let the stakeholders know in a way that the latter can understand the need for that change and embrace it.

- **Capturing necessary resources**

  Customers dislike spending money, and they definitely don't want to spend more than they deem necessary. However, if the team needs a resource, the project manager would be the one to fight to get it.

- **Managing conflict**

  This is another leadership skill that isn't limited to agile projects! It's inevitable that, when humans work together, there will be conflict. Whether it's among team members, or between the team and customer, a good project manager allows both sides to be heard, then helps everyone work together to find a solution. Project managers encourage healthy conflict within the team, so good ideas won't be buried under groupthink and members are free to speak up, even if they believe their opinion will be unpopular.

- **Preparing project plans**

  The project manager is responsible for developing the skeleton of the project that the team will work on. This is in conjunction with the stakeholders to ensure the latter's requirements are met.

- **Developing risk management plans**

  Similarly, the project manager looks ahead to see if any known risks are on the horizon. They would then prepare contingency plans that can be deployed if one of the risks does show up. As we discussed in chapter one, the opportunity is simply the other side of the coin from risk. A good project manager needs to take advantage of any opportunities that come their way as well.

- **Take care of any obstacles to completing on time**

  Obstacles don't just come in time and money form. It could be the departure of a team member or difficulty with a key stakeholder. Whatever it is, the buck stops with the project manager. They will be the ones who are ultimately responsible for keeping everything on track.

Common Issues with Project Management

The Project Management Institute Research (PMIR) estimates that $122 million is wasted for every $1 billion in projects in the United States due to a lack of project performance (Project Management Institute [PMI], 2020).[32] When managing a project, you are trying to minimize and contain the risk associated with it.

A project might take too long or be stopped abruptly. In other cases, it may not deliver the promised results or come in at budget. There are several factors responsible for these failures. When planning your project, you must account for every failure factor that can decide the fate of the project, which include:

- Poor communication between team members.
- Disunity amongst team members.
- Unrealistic expectations and projections.
- Poor planning and execution.
- Incompetence on the part of the project manager or team members.

You may have noticed that many of these are within your control. Some of them are not; every once in a while, two or more professionals can get into such a disagreement that they can no longer work together. However, for the most part, these issues can be prevented through proper planning and communication, along with good leadership.

Remember the 7 P's of the British Army: Proper Prior Planning Prevents Piss-Poor Performance. Knowing the plan ahead of time is key to success. If your team members are adequately prepared for their tasks and everyone is communicating well with each other, you will be unlikely to face a project failure.

Who Can Be a Great Project Manager?

As you saw from the list of responsibilities above, it's not necessarily certifications, credentials, or subject matter expertise that makes a project manager. It's their ability to lead a team.

Leading a team means that anyone can be a great project manager as long as they have leadership capabilities. Think about your own strengths—are you good at communicating with all kinds of people? Are you strong in your ability to manage conflict between others? Can you envision things from a bird's eye view? Are you a good coach? Can you motivate people? Is it easy for you to see which items to prioritize? Are you adaptable to change? It's rare for one person to have all these skills, but anyone or more of them will help you lead successful projects as a project manager.

Now that you've read this entire book, you should have gained a solid grasp of what agile and project management are all about. When you think back on what you've read, what character traits do you have that work well with what you've learned? What values do you have that fit right into the agile methodology? Considering these questions will help you become an ideal project manager. In the next book, we'll talk more about being an effective one, but for now, see how your personality fits into the lead role, no matter your education or current title.

Improving Your Skills as a Project Manager

You will want to be the best project manager you can be, so here are some ways you can improve your leadership skills. Many of these items are either enhanced by doing more and more projects, so you would learn and improve naturally over time, or by reading how others handled similar situations and succeeded or failed. A strong work ethic and desire for improvement will take you a long way.

- **Keep projects simple**

What's the simplest way to do a task that will achieve the result you want? Learn to look for inefficiencies. You and the team should always be asking yourselves if there's a better and more efficient way to do a task. Most people think that overcomplicating things will ensure the best results but the opposite is true! Great achievements are usually the result of being focused on one simple idea and eliminating the waste around it.

- **Continually improve project planning**

The more projects you manage, the better you'll become at planning them. Write whatever lessons you've learned from one project down, so you can have them for the next, and building on them as you go. You can find theories about planning projects that can help you get started, but you will improve as long as you implement what you've learned from previous projects into the new ones.

- **Control projects: maintain budgets and timelines, limit scope creep**

You'll be working on budgets and timelines with your team, so the experienced members will be able to validate whether the plan is too ambitious or not. The great thing about agile project management is that the iterations are relatively short, so you'll find out quickly if the plan is too ambitious. Once you do, you can then correct it immediately.

Scope creep is something you'll probably face from both the customer and your team while they discover new things during the project's process. It's a matter of you being able to hold the line and always think about what was initially promised.

- **Improve risk management**

  You can read about risk management to get started as a project manager, but this is another skill that you'll improve over time, as long as you continue to learn through previous projects. You'll have a better grasp of potential risks that can pop up, so your mitigation plans will become more effective over time.

- **Learn to be a good diplomat**

  Managing conflict falls mostly on you as the project manager. You'll probably have issues within the team and between the team and the customer. It's natural to have disagreements. You'll also need to build trust with the customer. Allowing both sides to be heard and finding a solution is key. Customers might get upset that the team isn't working exactly the way they think it should, or they may be pressuring the team in a way that makes the team less efficient. As a project manager, you'll need to take care of these situations without ruffling too many feathers on either side.

  You'll learn this on the job, but you can practice outside it as well! Do you belong to a sports league, or maybe the PTA at your child's school? Volunteer somewhere? If you belong to any kind of group, take the opportunity to work on being diplomatic whenever you can. If you look for opportunities, you will find them!

- **Communicate changes to the team as soon as you can**

  The team needs to know ASAP when things change, so they can prepare themselves. It may be a change in the stakeholders, the technology, whatever.

- **Set appropriate expectations and abide by them**

  We've discussed at length that team members need to be mature to do agile work because they would organize themselves to get

the work done. Make sure the team knows what you expect of them; they should understand it correctly, so there's no room for miscommunication and misunderstanding. If a team member isn't doing what they're supposed to do, you will need to call them out on it, though not necessarily in front of the whole team.

- **Organize your space and work**

  Whether you find tidying up fun or not, it is a fact that an organized workspace makes it much easier for the work to get done. In a tidy workspace, no one has to spend time looking for the resources they need, and it's much more calming to come in to work at a clean desk rather than a disastrous one.

  Similarly, organized work makes life much easier. Everyone knows what to do and when to do it, and there are no questions about what comes next or where to find any needed resources.

- **Be creative**

  You know APM is all about flexibility and adaptability, so being creative would be a vital trait of a good project manager. You can improve this outside the office by doing whatever creative projects bring you joy: crafting, woodworking, etc. You can also get creative by changing up a habit, like the route you normally drive to work in the morning. Drive in a different way and notice what's changed. You could also spend more time outdoors or listen to or create your own music.

- **Think critically**

  Being able to make decisions in the face of uncertainty and tackling problems confidently are also important for project managers.

  If you're not already in the habit of thinking this way, there are some games and articles that will help you. The three habits that will help you improve are questioning assumptions, reasoning through things logically, and looking at the situation from a different viewpoint.

You can practice these anywhere. When you're reading an article online, find the assumptions, then question them. Is the argument logical? What would be the opposing viewpoint? The more you practice—as with most skills—the better you'll become.

Key Takeaways

The role of a project manager is one of being a leader: having the ability to communicate with a variety of people, motivate and coach a team, help a team solve problems, develop a plan, and mitigate risks. These traits and skills aren't based on specific educational attainments or titles, but on the project manager as a leader. Anyone can be a project manager who is committed to improving their leadership skills.

- Leadership skills are more important than technical ones.
- There are a variety of certifications available for agile project managers, depending on the framework they prefer to use.
- Project managers are responsible mainly for leadership duties, not technical work.
- Anyone can be a great project manager, as long as they have leadership abilities.
- Most of the skills project managers need are soft ones, and there are a variety of ways to improve them, mainly participating and leading more projects.

[32] https://www.pmi.org

READY
SET
AGILE!

FINAL WORDS

AT this point in the journey, you have now learned that you have the capabilities to become a solid project manager for agile teams. You've got a thorough understanding of agile and its capabilities, and how you may personally put them to work on an agile team. Whether you were previously a traditional project manager, participated on some projects, or are new to this field, you can see that leadership strengths are essential to successful projects.

We discussed traditional project management—or waterfall—where the project is planned, start to finish, before any of the work begins. Each phase must also be completed before the next one can begin. The estimation and acquisition of necessary resources are also completed before work has started. Traditional tools such as Gantt charts are often deployed, though they may be digital to cut down on some of the manual work.

Project managers organize the teams, and the game plan is then laid out in sequential steps. Team members are typically experts in just one thing and may not work on the project for periods of time if the phase does not require them. The customer would provide most of the information for the planning stage and, once the project is in motion, rarely interact with the team beyond status updates.

Waterfall PM is still in use today because certain projects require the linear, preplanned nature of the method, such as with constructing bridges or office buildings. However, given how fast the modern world moves, it's unsuitable for many other applications. These projects can last for many months, only to find that the deliverable isn't what the customer wanted or currently needs.

This is where agile steps in. You've learned that it's designed to be adaptable and flexible so that if requirements or certain circumstances change during the project, they can be adopted into the process. There are different frameworks within agile, but they are all based on the Agile Manifesto and its twelve principles.

Because changes are common and frequent, the customer and other stakeholders are invited to participate in the meetings and provide feedback. All team members are tasked with communicating with each other, along with the client. They would also organize themselves, working on whatever is the next highest priority. Each team can be between three to nine members because they are cross-functional and don't have to wait for *their* phase to begin to start work.

At the beginning of the project, the team and stakeholders would put together the loose framework for the entire project, though not the entire step-by-step plan. Agile work takes place in shorter iterations or sprints, which may last from one week to one month. At the beginning of each sprint, the team—and sometimes stakeholders—plan out the work for that specific iteration, with the intent of releasing a feature that will appear in the final product. The customer has something to push out to their clients, so they can bring their product to market faster. At the end of the sprint, the team and customer conduct a review to see what went well and what could be improved.

While working, the team comes together for a daily stand-up. Each member would explain what they worked on the previous day and what's planned for the next. Stakeholders are often invited to these as well. They have visibility into the whole project, and they also have a better understanding of why one feature may take longer than another or than expected.

APM requires much more collaboration than the traditional method, and there are graphical charts that different frameworks would use for their projects, such as Kanban boards or burndown charts. Agile software applications are more sophisticated than their waterfall counterparts because they need to account for teams that may not be co-located, but still, need to work and meet together. There are a handful of popular applications out there. Although each has its advantages and disadvantages, if your team is already working with one type, there's usually no reason to change it. Starting anew, you may need to weigh the features and pick one that's right for your project.

Agile projects started in software development, which is an industry known for rapid change. However, many other sectors, including Fortune 500 companies, have adopted agile too so they can market faster. Agile has also moved beyond software development into new product development, marketing, customer service, and other functional areas within the corporation.

There are several agile frameworks to work with, and each of which has its way of organizing teams and work—and their own focus— while abiding by the twelve principles of the Agile Manifesto. You would choose a different framework based on whether you were trying to eliminate waste and inefficiencies, develop a new product, etc. You may also find that your own natural strengths will lead you to one framework over another.

Although there are certifications that you can earn, most of the skills you need for any framework are based on experience and leadership, as opposed to specific academic degrees or titles. These are called soft skills, and include communicating with people up and down the corporate ladder, motivating and coaching a team, and handling conflicts. The more agile projects you have under your belt, the stronger your leadership skills will become, as long as you are continually implementing the teachings from each sprint to every project.

My next book will go into more detail about being an effective project manager. But, for now, I hope you have gained the confidence to be an agile project manager and can start taking the steps you need to get there.

LEAVE A REVIEW

I would be incredibly *thankful* if you could take just 60 seconds to write a brief review on Amazon, even if it's just a few sentences.

If you have downloaded the *7 Best Practices of the Agile Project Manager Checklist* (the link is at the beginning of the book), you can take a photo, attach it to the review and share your experience. Your notes marked on the checklist will inspire and encourage many readers who may struggle in some areas.

Please log in to your Amazon account, then find this book *Become an Agile Project Manager* and create your review.

Alternatively, type this link into your browser, or scan the QR code:
www.amazon.com/dp/B08J1STMLD

Customer Reviews

51

4.8 out of 5 stars ▾

5 star	94%
4 star	2%
3 star	0%
2 star	2%
1 star	2%

See all 51 customer reviews ▸

Share your thoughts with other customers

Write a customer review

REFERENCES

Agile Alliance. (2019, September 24). **What is Extreme Programming (XP)?** Retrieved April 20, 2020, from https://www.agilealliance.org/glossary/xp/

Agile manifesto. (n.d.). **History: The Agile Manifesto.** Retrieved April 21, 2020, from https://agilemanifesto.org/history.html

Agile Manifesto. (n.d.). **Principles behind the Agile Manifesto.** Retrieved April 21, 2020, from https://agilemanifesto.org/principles.html

Alexander, M. (2018, June 19). **Agile project management: 12 key principles, 4 big hurdles.** Retrieved April 21, 2020, from https://www.cio.com/article/3156998/agile-project-management-a-beginners-guide.html

AltexSoft. (n.d.). **25 Scrum Process Best Practices That Set Your Agile Workflow for Efficiency.** Retrieved April 17, 2020, from https://www.altexsoft.com/blog/business/25-scrum-process-best-practices-that-set-your-agile-workflow-for-efficiency/

Ambler, S. (n.d.). **2013 IT Project Success Rates Survey Results.** Retrieved April 14, 2020, from http://www.ambysoft.com/surveys/success2013.html

ASQ. (n.d.). **Control Chart - Statistical Process Control Charts.** Retrieved April 20, 2020, from https://asq.org/quality-resources/control-chart

Association For Project Management. (n.d.). **What is project management?** Retrieved April 4, 2020, from https://www.apm.org.uk/resources/what-is-project-management/

Aston, B. (2020, April 21). **Essential Project Management Skills And Traits for 2020.** Retrieved April 24, 2020, from https://thedigitalprojectmanager.com/project-management-skills/

Atlassian. (n.d.). **Scrum**. Retrieved April 17, 2020, from https://www.atlassian.com/agile/scrum

Banerjee, S. (2016, August 12). **Role of Project Manager in Managing Agile Projects.** Retrieved April 23, 2020, from https://www.hilarispublisher.com/open-access/role-of-a-project-manager-in-managing-agile-projects-2167-0234-1000204.pdf

Berger, H. (2007). **Agile development in a bureaucratic arena—A case study experience. International Journal of Information Management,** 27(6), 386–396. https://doi.org/10.1016/j.ijinfomgt.2007.08.009

Brocchi, C. (2016, December 1). **Using agile to accelerate your data transformation.** Retrieved April 14, 2020, from https://www.mckinsey.com/business-functions/mckinsey-digital/our-insights/using-agile-to-accelerate-your-data-transformation

Capterra. (n.d.-a). **Agile Project Management Tools Software.** Retrieved April 14, 2020, from https://www.capterra.com/agile-project-management-tools-software/

Capterra. (n.d.-b). **JIRA Reviews and Pricing.** Retrieved April 14, 2020, from https://www.capterra.com/p/19319/JIRA/

Chandana. (2019, October 4). **Scrum Project Management.** Retrieved April 17, 2020, from https://www.simplilearn.com/scrum-project-management-article

Ciccarelli, D. (2018, August 7). **When to Use Agile Project Management: The Definitive Guide.** Retrieved April 22, 2020, from https://www.goskills.com/Project-Management/Articles/When-to-use-agile-project-management

Cohn, M. (n.d.). **Ten Sentences With All the Scrum Master Advice You'll Ever Need.** Retrieved April 17, 2020, from https://www.mountaingoatsoftware.com/blog/ten-sentences-with-all-the-scrum-master-advice-youll-ever-need

Cohn, M. & Keith, C. (2018, August 31). **How To Fail With Agile.** Retrieved April 23, 2020, from https://www.mountaingoatsoftware.com/articles/how-to-fail-with-agile

Dey, S. (n.d.). **Why Should You Choose Six Sigma?** Retrieved April 20, 2020, from https://www.greycampus.com/blog/quality-management/why-should-you-choose-six-sigma

Digite. (2020, April 3). **What Is Kanban? An Overview Of The Kanban Method.** Retrieved April 19, 2020, from https://www.digite.com/kanban/what-is-kanban/

Dogma Systems. (2017, January 20). **Scrum - A Framework or a Methodology.** Retrieved April 16, 2020, from https://www.dogmasystems.com/scrum-framework-or-methodology/

Dutton, G. (2018, March 29). **Choosing the Right Agile Strategy.** Retrieved April 20, 2020, from https://trainingmag.com/trgmag-article/choosing-right-agile-strategy/

Edwards, J. (2017, October 25). **7 simple ways to fail at agile.** Retrieved April 21, 2020, from https://www.cio.com/article/3234366/7-simple-ways-to-fail-at-agile.html

Francino, Y. (2019, January 22). **How to use agile techniques to manage your personal life.** Retrieved April 22, 2020, from https://techbeacon.com/app-dev-testing/personal-scrum-using-agile-techniques-manage-your-life

Freeman, J. (2020, January 31). **8 Project Management Tools You Should Know.** Retrieved April 4, 2020, from https://www.edrawsoft.com/project-management-tools.html

Gonçalves, L. (2019, March 26). **Understanding the Scrum Pillars: Transparency, Inspection and Adaptation.** Retrieved April 16, 2020, from https://luis-goncalves.com/scrum-pillars/

Harris, A. (2013, October 30). **6 unexpected ways Six Sigma can benefit your company.** Retrieved April 20, 2020, from https://www.processexcellencenetwork.com/lean-six-sigma-business-performance/articles/6-ways-six-sigma-can-benefit-your-company

Harvard Business Review. (2016, November 3). **Five Critical Roles in Project Management.** Retrieved April 5, 2020, from https://hbr.org/2016/11/five-critical-roles-in-project-management

Hasan, S. (2019, August 8). **PMBoK Knowledge Areas: 9 Must Know Aspects Related to PM.** Retrieved April 4, 2020, from https://blog.taskque.com/pmbok-knowledge-areas/

Hiscock, A. J. (2016, August 15). **How Fortune 500 Companies Transform "Agile" From Buzzword to Business Model.** Retrieved April 14, 2020, from https://www.business2community.com/business-innovation/fortune-500-companies-transform-agile-buzzword-business-model-01625695

Howard, L. (2018, June 5). **Planit - Why is Scrum So Popular?** Retrieved April 16, 2020, from https://www.planittesting.com/uk/insights/2018/why-is-scrum-so-popular

IPMA. (n.d.). **History of IPMA.** Retrieved April 14, 2020, from https://www.ipma.world/about-us/ipma-international/history-of-ipma/

Johnson, E. (2015, January 23). **Lessons Learned from Failures of Agile Development.** Retrieved April 23, 2020, from https://content.intland.com/blog/agile/failure-of-agile

Kumar, P. (2020, April 13). **What is Six Sigma: A Complete Overview.** Retrieved April 19, 2020, from https://www.simplilearn.com/what-is-six-sigma-a-complete-overview-article

Lazarow, A. (2020, March 26). **Why you may still be working from home after the coronavirus crisis is over.** Retrieved April 16, 2020, from https://www.marketwatch.com/story/why-you-may-still-be-working-from-home-after-the-coronavirus-crisis-is-over-2020-03-26

Lesue, D. (2018, May 7). **The Beginners' Guide to Agile Project Management Methodology.** Retrieved April 5, 2020, from https://www.workfront.com/blog/the-beginners-guide-to-agile-project-management-methodology

Lucidchart. (2018, September 5). **What the Waterfall Project Management Methodology Can (and Can't) Do for You.** Retrieved April 5, 2020, from https://www.lucidchart.com/blog/waterfall-project-management-methodology

Lynn, R. (2019, November 21). **Agile Best Practices for More Effective Teams.** Retrieved April 21, 2020, from https://www.planview.com/resources/guide/agile-methodologies-a-beginners-guide/agile-best-practices-effective-teams/

Lynn, R. (2020a, January 24). **Project Portfolio Management Defined.** Retrieved April 14, 2020, from https://www.planview.com/resources/guide/project-management-office-ppm-best-practices/project-portfolio-management-defined/

Lynn, R. (2020, January 30). **Kanban vs. Scrum: What are the Differences?** Retrieved April 19, 2020, from https://www.planview.com/resources/articles/kanban-vs-scrum/

Lynn, R. (2020, March 11). **Disadvantages of Agile.** Retrieved April 14, 2020, from https://www.planview.com/resources/articles/disadvantages-agile/

Lynn, R. (2020, March 26). **What is Scrumban?** Retrieved April 19, 2020, from https://www.planview.com/resources/articles/lkdc-what-is-scrumban/

Mersino, A. (2018, April 1). **Project Success Rates: Agile vs. Waterfall.** Retrieved April 14, 2020, from https://vitalitychicago.com/blog/agile-projects-are-more-successful-traditional-projects/

Military Wiki (n.d.). **7 Ps (military adage)** Retrieved April 4, 2020, from https://military.wikia.org/wiki/7_Ps_(military_adage)

Moujib, A. (n.d.). **Lean Project Management.** Retrieved April 19, 2020, from https://www.pmi.org/learning/library/lean-project-management-7364

Mountain Goat Software. (n.d.). **User Stories.** Retrieved April 17, 2020, from https://www.mountaingoatsoftware.com/agile/user-stories

Mrsic, M. (2017, April 5). **Project Manager Roles and Responsibilities [8 Key Roles].** Retrieved April 5, 2020, from https://activecollab.com/blog/project-management/project-manager-roles-and-responsibilities

National Audit Office. (2019, June 4). **Universal Credit: early progress - National Audit Office (NAO) Report.** Retrieved April 23, 2020, from https://www.nao.org.uk/report/universal-credit-early-progress-2/

Nielson, N. (2013, July 5). **Growing Up Agile - How Popular is this Teenage Methodology?** Retrieved April 5, 2020, from https://dzone.com/articles/growing-agile-how-popular

Novoseltseva, E. (2020, February 19). **5 benefits of agile project management you must know about.** Retrieved April 14, 2020, from https://apiumhub.com/tech-blog-barcelona/benefits-of-agile-project-management/

Olic, A. (2017, June 21). **Advantages and disadvantages of Agile Project Management [Checklist].** Retrieved April 14, 2020, from https://activecollab.com/blog/project-management/agile-project-management-advantages-disadvantages

Olic, A. (2017, May 24). **Waterfall Project Management Methodology.** Retrieved April 5, 2020, from https://activecollab.com/blog/project-management/waterfall-project-management-methodology

Pahuja, S. (2017, June 22). **What is Scrumban?** Retrieved April 19, 2020, from https://www.agilealliance.org/what-is-scrumban/

Pitagorsky, G. (n.d.). **Agile and Lean Project Management.** Retrieved April 19, 2020, from https://www.pmi.org/learning/library/agile-lean-project-management-formality-7992

Planview. (n.d.). **Scrum Best Practices for Teams.** Retrieved April 17, 2020, from https://www.planview.com/resources/articles/scrum-best-practices-teams/

Project Management Institute. (n.d.). **Certifications.** Retrieved April 5, 2020, from https://www.pmi.org/certifications

Project Manager. (n.d.). **Waterfall Methodology - Tools and Strategies.** Retrieved April 14, 2020, from https://www.projectmanager.com/software/use-cases/waterfall-methodology

PwC. (2017, July 1). **Agile Project Delivery Confidence.** Retrieved April 5, 2020, from https://www.pwc.com/us/en/services/risk-assurance/library/agile-project-delivery-methodology.html

Rajpal, M. (2016, May 24). **Lessons Learned from a Failed Attempt at Distributed Agile.** Retrieved April 23, 2020, from https://link.springer.com/chapter/10.1007/978-3-319-33515-5_21

Rayome, A. D. (2018, April 17). **How to tell if Agile is the right project management style for your business.** Retrieved April 22, 2020, from https://www.techrepublic.com/article/how-to-tell-if-agile-is-the-right-project-management-style-for-your-business/

Sabatowski, K. (2019, December 5). **7 Agile best practices you should know.** Retrieved April 21, 2020, from https://sunscrapers.com/blog/agile-software-development-7-best-practices/

Santana, J. (2019, February 28). **How to Know If Agile Is Right for You.** Retrieved April 22, 2020, from https://www.projectmanager.com/blog/know-agile-right

Schauder, J. (2016, September 30). **Work Breakdown Structure Versus Backlog.** Retrieved April 17, 2020, from http://blog.schauderhaft.de/2016/09/30/workbreakdownstructure-vs-backlog/

Scrum Alliance. (n.d.). **Certified ScrumMaster® (CSM®) Certification Course.** Retrieved April 23, 2020, from https://www.scrumalliance.org/get-certified/scrum-master-track/certified-scrummaster

Scrum.org. (n.d.). **What is a Product Owner?** Retrieved April 17, 2020, from https://www.scrum.org/resources/what-is-a-product-owner

Scrum.org. (n.d.). **What is a Scrum Development Team?** Retrieved April 17, 2020, from https://www.scrum.org/resources/what-is-a-scrum-development-team

Sergeev, A. (2018, June 22). **Roles in Waterfall Methodology.** Retrieved April 5, 2020, from https://hygger.io/blog/team-roles-in-waterfall-methodology/

Siroky, D. (2020, March 6). **Agile and DevOps are failing in Fortune 500 companies.** Retrieved April 22, 2020, from https://www.plutora.com/blog/agile-devops-failing-fortune-500-companies-wake-call-us

Smartsheet. (n.d.). **Waterfall.** Retrieved April 5, 2020, from https://www.smartsheet.com/content-center/best-practices/project-management/project-management-guide/waterfall-methodology

Spilker, J. (2018, June 7). **How To Improve Your Project Management: Success Strategies from Workzone.** Retrieved April 24, 2020, from https://www.workzone.com/blog/how-to-improve-project-management/

Sutherland, J. (2019, May 29). **A Tale of Two Scrums: Agile Done Right and Agile Gone Wrong.** Retrieved April 22, 2020, from https://openviewpartners.com/blog/agile-done-right-agile-gone-wrong/#.XqClIJlIA2w

Synerzip. (2019, July 29). **4 Examples of Agile in Non-technology Businesses.** Retrieved April 22, 2020, from https://www.synerzip.com/blog/4-examples-of-agile-in-non-technology-businesses/

Townsend, J. (2013, February 7). **Why Is Scrum So Popular?** Retrieved April 16, 2020, from https://www.techwell.com/2013/02/why-scrum-so-popular

Velasquez, S. (2020, February 18). **Agile Development in the Real World.** Retrieved April 22, 2020, from https://www.growthaccelerationpartners.com/blog/agile-development-real-world/

Verheyen, G. (2019, February 22). **There's value in the Scrum Values.** Retrieved April 16, 2020, from https://guntherverheyen.com/2013/05/03/theres-value-in-the-scrum-values/

Visual Paradigm. (n.d.). **What Are Scrum Artifacts?** Retrieved April 17, 2020, from https://www.visual-paradigm.com/scrum/what-are-scrum-artifacts/

Visual Paradigm. (n.d.). **What is a Scrum Master? The Roles and Responsibilities.** Retrieved April 17, 2020, from https://www.visual-paradigm.com/scrum/what-is-scrum-master/

VivifyScrum. (2019, March 15). **What is Lean Agile Project Management?** Retrieved April 19, 2020, from https://www.vivifyscrum.com/insights/lean-agile-project-management

Watson, Z. (2019, August 20). **The Best Project Management Tools for (Almost) Any Task.** Retrieved April 4, 2020, from https://technologyadvice.com/blog/information-technology/5-of-the-best-project-management-tools-for-almost-any-task/

Wikipedia contributors. (2020, March 15). **Six Sigma.** Retrieved April 19, 2020, from https://en.wikipedia.org/wiki/Six_Sigma

Wilson, F. (2020, January 25). **Agile Best Practices Every Agile Team Should Have in Place.** Retrieved April 21, 2020, from https://www.ntaskmanager.com/blog/agile-best-practices/

Wrike. (n.d.). **Popular Agile Project Management Frameworks.** Retrieved April 20, 2020, from https://www.wrike.com/project-management-guide/project-management-frameworks/

GLOSSARY AND ABBREVIATIONS

Agile/APM: Agile Project Management, methodology, or framework ..... ch. 3

Agile Manifesto: 12 core values of APM defined in 2001 ..... ch. 8

Aging Work in Progress: How much work is not being done or aging ..... ch. 3

CAPM: The Certified Associate in Project Management ..... ch. 10

Cycle Time: Time spent working on a given process item ..... ch. 3

Daily Meetings: Short meetings with the team each morning ..... ch. 3

Development Team: All members of the Scrum project team ..... ch. 6

DMAIC: Define, Measure, Analyze, Improve, Control (Six Sigma) ..... ch. 7

DMADV: Define, Measure, Analyze, Design, Validate (Six Sigma) ..... ch. 7

Framework: Describes how to achieve a goal following a methodology ..... ch. 7

Gantt Chart: A visual scheduling diagram named by Henry Gantt ..... ch. 1

HR: Human Resources ..... ch. 1

Increment: The sum of all backlog items completed during a sprint ..... ch. 6

Integration Management: Managing different parts of a project ..... ch. 1

IT: Information Technology (software, hardware, and solutions) ..... ch. 3

Kanban: APM method for improving workflow, uses visual tools ..... ch. 7

Kanban Board: A visual board with tasks separated into status lines ..... ch. 7

Lead Time: How long it takes from the client request to deliver the item ..... ch. 3

Lean: A process improvement framework, seeks to eliminate waste ..... ch. 7

Lean Six Sigma: Combination of Lean and Six Sigma APM frameworks ..... ch. 7

Methodology: Outlines PM principles, values, and best practices ..... ch. 7

Mind Map: Generating and mapping ideas visually ..... ch. 1

OPM3: Organizational Project Management Maturity Model ..... ch. 7

PERT: Project Evaluation and Review Technique chart ..... ch. 1

Plus/EBIs: Plus and Even Better Ifs (APM improvement practice) ..... ch. 8

PM: Project Management ..... ch. 1

PMI: Project Management Institute ..... ch. 10

PMP: Project Management Professional, certification ..... ch. 10

PPM: Project Portfolio Management (management of all projects) ..... ch. 4

Process: Activities performed repetitively .... ch. 1

Product Backlog: Captures the features and deliverables for each sprint .... ch. 5

Product Owner: Maximizes product value, updates the product backlog .... ch. 6

Project: An effort to create something new or modify .... ch. 1

Project Manager: Leads the project and project team .... ch. 1

Prototype: A deliverable that may not be complete or fully functional .... ch. 3

QA: Quality Assurance .... ch. 1

Ready, Set, Agile!: Methodology for planning and executing projects .... ch. 5

Review Meeting: Held after each sprint to evaluate how it went .... ch. 6

Risk Management: Foreseeing and addressing potential risks .... ch. 1

ROI: Return on Investment (return per dollar invested in the project) .... ch. 3

Scope Creep: Continuously adding new deliverables to the scope .... ch. 1

Scrum: The most popular APM method for developing complex products .... ch. 6

Scrum Board: A board with tasks divided into status columns .... ch. 6

Scrum Master: A coach, promotes productivity, can be a project manager .... ch. 6

Scrum Meeting: Short daily meetings or stand-ups .... ch. 6

Scrumban: A combined agile framework from Scrum and Kanban .... ch. 7

Seven P's: Proper Prior Planning Prevents Piss-Poor Performance .... ch. 10

Six Sigma: A process improvement framework, using statistics measures .... ch. 7

Sponsor: Has have the most significant interest in the project's outcome .... ch. 1

Sprint: An iteration or cycle in the APM that lasts about a month .... ch. 3

Sprint Backlog: Tasks from the product backlog for the current sprint .... ch. 6

Stage Planning: A high-level calendar for what features will be released .... ch. 3

Stakeholder: Has "stake" in the outcome of the project .... ch. 1

Subcontractor: An outside contractor who develops a portion of the project .... ch. 1

SWOT: Strengths, Weaknesses, Opportunities, Threats .... ch. 7

Throughput: How much work is completed compared to the time used .... ch. 3

User Story: Explains each feature and its importance to the user .... ch. 6

Waterfall: A traditional PM methodology, the chart resembles a waterfall .... ch. 2

WBS: Work Breakdown Structure (a tree structure with activities) .... ch. 1

WIP: Work in Progress .... ch. 7

XP: Extreme Programming, an APM framework for software development .... ch. 7

BECOME AN AGILE
PROJECT MANAGER

2020

Made in the USA
Las Vegas, NV
23 November 2022